To Jane

To Jayne
a great biology
teacher & writer

Ann Berger

1

Everybody's Good for Something

by

Ann Berger

Honoring our parents Louis and Frieda Gehrke

With gratitude to my nine siblings:

HelenVelmaBerniceDonna
PaulLilasLoisMarilynMeredith

Who put in their two cents

There will be no test

Cover: Oil painting by Ann Berger

Table of Contents

Lady of the House

Doc Woodruff slapped my bottom at 4:32 a.m. on March 20,1923. Later that same year President Harding died on August 3. Vice President Calvin Coolidge was wakened from his sleep in Vermont to be sworn in as our 30th President by lamplight by his father, a notary public.

At midnight, in March in Minnesota, Louis Gehrke had been roused by Frieda's "It's time." He stumbled out of their feather bed to rouse his white mare, Lady, from her pile of straw. He tacked up the mare for the eight-mile horseback trip to fetch the doctor. Man and mare bowed their groggy heads in obeisance to a Minnesota blizzard.

Doc Woodruff, with his sorrel gelding hitched to his cutter, bucked over and through snowdrifts squinting to keep a bead on that white mare and rider blazing their trail back to my birthplace on County Road 74. They arrived in time to help Frieda deal with her issue; giving birth to a ten-pound daughter—her fifth.

That mare, Lady, had been the driving force in Louis' courting days. After an evening out, he'd take Frieda home, loop the reins over the buggy-whip holder, settle under his cowhide robe for a nap and wake up at the door of his own barn.

Blue-eyed blonde Frieda Krumdieck grew up attracting flirtations from Louis, the brown-haired lad across the aisle in parochial school. Her parents, Henry and Mary, fended off what they viewed as a dubious dalliance for their nubile daughter by sending her across the state line to pursue a career in fashion design and pattern making. Between stitches, she became bewitched by sandy-haired George.

The minute she returned from school in Wisconsin, Louis hitched up Lady to replace interloper George in Frieda's affections. While President Woodrow Wilson was busy leading our country in World War I, Louis led this 19-year-old lass to the altar on September

19, 1917. He took his bride home to his widowed father, Ernest Gehrke, on the "home place" where she became "The Lady of the House."

She was a born mother. Her dowry of gentle optimism mixed with Louis' sly humor muffled sounds of us children playing and squabbling to grow up. Together they embraced her destiny of motherhood. The final score: one boy and nine girls.

Throughout our lives she forged a comfort zone for each us with three girls to a double bed, and the boy sharing a room with Grandpa G. Her motto: "A place for everyone and everyone in his place."

Frieda's Fingers

Most people didn't notice Frieda's crooked fingers, some looked away. A team of runaway horses did it to her right hand. A runaway team had galloped from behind and crashed atop her family's buggy. Before her father, Henry Krumdieck, could rein his team out of the runaways' path, his family landed in the ditch with infant Frieda in her mother's arms. Except for the baby's injured fingers, no one was hurt beyond bruises and sore muscles. William and Charlie Mayo's Clinic had already been operating for twenty years, but that was twenty miles away on dirt roads. Baby Frieda was treated by their country doctor who made house calls.

Her picture, taken in 1905, shows Frieda "all dressed up with no place to go," as her father often teased when she came downstairs in her Sunday dress. Today she had a place to go. Henry had hitched the sorrel team, Cap and Prince, to the surrey to drive his family, to Spring Valley, Minnesota nine miles from their farm. Her mother, Mary, had made an appointment to have Frieda photographed at J. A. Stevens studio.

It seemed to Frieda that Mr. Stevens was playing hide and seek under a black cloth behind a big machine. He whispered, "Be perfectly still until after this long thing in my hand makes a light brighter than any gas lamp." Mary had assured her daughter that having her picture taken wouldn't hurt. She could pretend to be like the models in Sears Roebuck catalogs.

She posed "perfectly still" as did models of the time, which happened to be the era of Matisse initiating the new period of experimentation in France with his Woman in the Hat. Frieda wasn't wearing a hat; but then, Matisse's painting happened across the ocean and she had never seen the ocean. Her father, Henry, had left Europe by boat as a teenager after America's Civil War and wasn't about to return just to place his daughter into the fashionable art world.

Frieda twiddled with her fingers dreaming of spiffing up in a string of beads and a ring to travel, especially to THE wedding, she'd heard grownups talking about. Imagine! The President of the United States, Theodore Roosevelt, would be at the wedding.

His niece, Eleanor Roosevelt, was to marry her cousin, Franklin D. Roosevelt, in New York, wherever that was—-much too far for a horse and buggy ride she imagined. Go by train? Maybe, except she heard of a train wreck just last year in Colorado that killed 96 people and 56 had died in a train wreck in New Market, Tennessee. Flying really was a fantasy. Two years earlier, Wilbur and Orville Wright's heavier-than-air plane had lifted off the ground, but only the J. P. Morgan/Rockefeller families traveled that way. Or, by car? Henry Ford's first Tin Lizzy with creaks removed from crankshafts and gearshifts was already rolling off new-fangled assembly lines.

Frieda's family didn't have a Tin Lizzy. Her father's surrey suited her just fine. At least it was better than that damaged one-seat buggy they had been riding on that Sunday five years ago when the runaway team climbed atop their rig.

By and by, her crumpled fingers grew into question marks, but they soon learned to fly across keys of their Gulbrandson upright piano and Cornish pump organ during music lessons.

By the time the Big Depression hit, those fingers helped steer the jumping-bean needle on Frieda's Home treadle sewing machine to stitch dresses, coats, and underwear for her nine daughters as well as shirts and jackets for her son---right up to 1973 within weeks of her fingers resting to the strains of "The Lord is My Shepherd" at her graveside.

That same year, 1973, Englishman Housefield conceived the CT Scan, which may, or may not, have been able to turn her question-mark fingers into exclamation points.

Frieda age 5

Picture This

During house or barn dances, I let myself be mesmerized watching our parents glide round and round the dance floor every bit as graceful as those Old Smoothies waltzing on skates in the famous Ice Capades productions. After a swig or two, or five, of home brew, his finesse on the dance floor heightened into a virtuoso that had her leaning into his mood. Pure synergism.

Synchronizing their moods throughout life always seemed seamless. Whenever daily living threw them a curve, a shrug with knowing glances said, "we'll never know the difference a 100 years from now" lifting spirits throughout our family.

Ma's instincts for homemaking neared perfection. While she fretted at a chip in the baseboard one day, Pa leaned against a doorjamb, grinned and drawled, "hang a picture over it." His nonsensical fix-it response seeded itself, took root and sprouted into a full-blown family mantra.

No matter where the flaw, be it on the floor, a window, stair riser, or the ceiling, "hang a picture over it" was heard.

Her credence of his fix-it proposal found a home in her psyche; though frustration at times most certainly must have tempted her to let fly with mutterings sounding a lot like cheese'ncrackersgotallmuddy---which would never come from Frieda's mouth.

If a daughter whined about a petticoat peeking beneath a hem, one might hear, "hang a picture..." all the while Ma would already be closing in with needle and thread in hand. Skinned knees, insect bites, as well as our brother Paul's deviated septum after he fell out of a tree got "hang a picture over..." as she administered TLC in her homemade ER.

Embracing Louis' outlandish mantra turned many inevitable family accidents into mere happenings.

Shady Lady

The mare, Lady, became Ma's driving horse and belonged to any child willing to pet and climb all over her. I jumped at the chance. Lady was my chance to be alone since one father, one mother, eight sisters Helen, Velma, Bernice (Bee), Donna, Lilas, Lois, Marilyn, Meredith, one brother Paul, occasional hired men, Fred, Arlo, Hans, or Glen, and hired girls, Eleanor or Edna, interfered with my solitude.

Hiding in foliage of the lilac archway, or hunching under a blanket draped across two dining room chairs pulled into the shade of maple trees on the front lawn worked pretty well on cool days. I read and reread the book Whistling Rock. The last sentence is "Goodbye, Loveday, come back next summer" as the protagonist waves to her friend leaving the lake. Pure fantasy. Vacationing at a lake for us, even in this Land of 10,000 Lakes, seemed impossible–unthinkable.

Then I got lucky. A hailstorm shredded every stalk of corn, oats, barley and flax. Our parents turned away from the devastation and packed us into our touring Jewet with its isinglass side curtains.

We drove to Lake Pepin more than 50 miles north along the Wisconsin border and unpacked in a one-room cabin. Immediately, Pa turned the car around to go home alone to plow, harrow and drag to plant millet. He planned the millet should be ready to harvest in time for livestock feed before the first frost.

At the lake, I was in heaven stepping into the pages of Whistling Rock to find my very own Loveday, named Marvis Olson, with whom older sister Donna and I spent every day beach combing, splashing and taking a stab at swimming. We felt important when Marvis's mother asked us to pose for pictures on the beach. Forget that my knees stuck out like upturned teacups on my spindly legs---I WAS AT

THE BEACH. That week of living like the swells feeds my soul still.

That week in Paradise ended when Pa came to take us home. Our farm was still a mess. We unpacked. Ma climbed into men's bib overalls, picked up her straw hat, and a handful of reins.

She adeptly drove a four-in-hand team pulling the grain seeder with the skill of one of those drivers of Budweiser's popular parade team.

We children were impressed! But not so very impressed when it hit us that now we'd be chief cooks and bottle washers while Ma took up even heavier duties behind four horses pulling that grain seeder.

With trees and bushes still stripped of leaves, where could a girl find shade to read? I stalked the farm for a shady place to be alone in the shade with my book. Suddenly, there it was, in plain sight---under reliable Lady. Leaning against her legs and moving with the sun let me sit in her shade. Her switching tail brushed away flies. True, either of the big bays, Rex or

Hector, would have given more shade, but they were geldings who might have given me a warm shower. I reasoned that Lady, being white, would give cooler shade and behave naturally, like a lady.

Cooler shade or not, under her was a place to be alone right out in the open where no one tried to read over my shoulder.

Apart from being alone, under Lady gave more room to stretch out than I ever got while trying to read in my bed shared with two sisters.

Growing up sleeping three to a bed, had programmed me to wonder on my wedding night, "Where is everybody?"

Pegasus Pulling a U-Haul

One sunny autumn afternoon in 1931 when sister Donna was nearly ten, barely a year older than I, Ma offered us a choice chore. "Girls, how would you like to hitch up Lady and drive to Tante Vina's to borrow the sauerkraut cutter? Do you think you could do that?" Boy, could we! We flew off the back porch heading for the pasture. Her voice trailed after us, "Come back. You can't go looking like that. Wash up and put on clean dresses." But, we were already through the pasture gate to round up Lady.

Lickety split we had Lady tied in her stall. I boosted Donna to reach the driving harness and bridle. Lady dipped her nose to take the bit and lowered her head for me to fasten the buckle. Lifting the harness in place with all belts and straps buckled, we backed Lady into the fills of the buggy, hitched her tugs to the singletree, ground tied her and ran to the house to spiff up in clean dresses. In short order, we climbed into the buggy pulling our clean cotton dresses around our bare thighs in ladylike fashion to protect us from the hot leather bench-style seat.

Donna took the reins (her claim to being the elder) and drove off the yard turning right for the one-mile ride to Tante Vina's and Uncle Tader's, favorite relatives who had teenage, sophisticated cousins.

Rather than hanging around for chatter or the usual sweet treats, we stopped only long enough to secure the sauerkraut cutter in the trunk of the buggy. Grinning, we turned toward home in a glorious frenzy of having Lady all to ourselves. Past the Township Hall surrounded by a stand of trees we broke into the open and headed downhill.

"Let's go faster," I urged. Donna slapped the reins lightly on Lady's rump. Lady plodded. Donna slapped the reins again. Lady chose her own pace. We waved our arms hoping to startle her into going faster. Lady didn't take the hint. I slid off the seat and banged the flat of my hands against the dashboard. Lady leaped into a flat-out gallop.

At that very moment, Pa, disking in an adjacent field, also broke into the open to catch us doing an imitation of Pegasus pulling a U-Haul.

He didn't lay a hand on us–he never did. When he came in for supper he simply related the scene to Ma, who talked to us by hand---her exclusive privilege.

Thanks to Lisa Stange for this drawing.

How to Treat Lady

The next Christmas vacation, Donna and I were called to the barn in a no-nonsense tone, "Now that you've had time to think about how you mistreated Lady last fall, are you ready for some plain talk?" We knew this would not be a talking-to-by-hand session. That was Ma's bailiwick

Pa demonstrated how to approach Lady, how to groom her, pick her feet clean and how to feed her. We watched, listened and practiced reining her under his strict orders on what to do and what not to do. By Easter Sunday, satisfied with our trial runs holding the reins and our general demeanor around Lady, he thrilled us by asking us to drive Lady home alone after taking the big girls, Helen, Velma and Bee, back to their boarding school.

With their luggage stowed in the buggy trunk and the lid closed flat, comfortable seats were fashioned for

Donna and me. From there we could see where we had been.

Velma announced, "around the next corner is where my favorite new classmate Esther Duparee lives."

Bee said, "I like her new spring coat, don't you, Helen? Helen was too busy holding the reins to answer. Velma and Bee fell into discussing how some of the kids combed their hair, giggling about the preacher's son's pompadour.

After a few more miles, Helen steered Lady to the boarding place, Mrs. Broitzman's in Wykoff. The second Helen called "whoa" and pulled up on the reins, Donna and I slid off the trunk, dying for our chance on the front seat. Velma and Bee unpacked the trunk. And made sure luggage was safe on the sidewalk away from the buggy wheels. Helen checked buckles of the harness and bridle, handed Lady's head toward home saying, "Lady knows the way home." The big girls waved us toward the turn we should take to be on the graveled road. We were off.

Helen called out, "Don't let Lady run." Fat chance Donna would stage another Pegasus U-Haul show. Donna clicked her tongue to ask Lady to pick up the pace.

All she got was a shrug of Lady's shoulders. Donna's "giddyap" got a sassy flip of Lady's hips. Donna smirked. "I guess she heard those strict-orders-from-headquarters that we heard all winter."

Lady ignored our tongue clicking, and fussing at her to hurry up. Suddenly she stopped, of all places, in front of Kenny Marshall's home. We were mortified for fear Kenny, a teenager with the only racy car in the township, might see us poking along in the buggy.

"Should I bang on the dash board?"

"You better not" hissed Donna gripping the reins and glaring straight ahead. Lady' s ears twitched. Finally, dust billowed from several hilltops ahead. Presently, a car appeared. As soon as the car met us and passed by, Lady put herself in gear and sauntered on. Twice more her keen ears told her to stop, shift into idle, and wait for cars that she *knew* were coming. Each time as soon as the cars passed she went into gear.

While Lady was not spooked by cars, she did respect these occasional noisy intrusions on *her* country roads.

Without waiting for their dust to settle, she pleased herself and carried us through our farm gate well before dark where one relieved father waited with a bucket of oats.

Dust to Dust

For the most part, Lady took noisy, dust-raising cars, or rattle-trap pickups on our country roads in stride. She could outpace Henry Ford's model T's, or Tin Lizzies while new motorists fiddled with getting the hang of cranking and shouting instructions, "pull down the gas lever on the steering column, now let up on the foot feed" to a helper in the driver's seat. Once their engine fired up, Lady would already be leaving the cars in her dust while drivers puzzled out which foot to press when or where--the clutch or the foot feed, or both--to shift gears from idle, low, second and high. We children cheered for Lady.

It was generally understood that Helen chose to steer clear of horses. Cars were a different matter. Before she had reached legal age to drive a car, Pa bragged, "if it's got four wheels, Helen can drive it." The hired man, Arlo, had questioned this 11-year-old lass climbing behind the steering wheel of the old Dodge pickup.

With Arlo shaking his head, Helen was off the barnyard headed for the back forty to pick up a load of fencing.

Cars were a welcome respite in our daily rural life. When the call rang out "Car Coming!" we scrambled to the front windows (unless it was meal time). If we happened to be out-of-doors, we dropped everything, whether it be a hoe in the garden, wet laundry at the clothesline, or pails of drinking water being carried to the house. We'd gather on the front lawn to salute the motorist of the moment.

There was no mistaking when 'Speed' Kenny was heading our way by the sounds he made gunning the motor of his sporty car. Housewives dreaded his dusty trail, slammed shut their front windows and hoped he wouldn't go to town on Mondays before they had taken their laundry off the clotheslines.

Hanging laundry was an art. Neatness counted. White and light colors hung in the sun, darks in the shade of the orchard, maples or smokehouse.

Sheets were hung with sheets, shirts with shirts, socks, socks, underwear, underwear, etc. One neighbor went beyond neatness all the way to modesty. She hung unmentionables inside pillowslips.

Sounds of airplane motors were a different matter, for them we were allowed to leave the dinner or supper table in a race to be the first to spot those intriguing machines slipping from behind fluffy clouds in our smog-free summer skies of Minnesota. We were proud to learn that Charles Lindbergh was a native of Minnesota.

Then came that hushed late fall morning when our blue skies faded to a bleak overcast. The merry sound of Pa's whistling or singing "Now the Moon Shines Tonight on Pretty Red Wing" floated through the heating register in our bedroom where, for more than a week now, we had snuggled under patch-work quilts, three to a bed, with various stages of Chicken Pox. He was firing up the furnace before going to the barn for morning chores. We turned over to snooze waiting for him to come back in for breakfast and for Ma's call "time to get up," or for her to appear with trays for those of us too feverish to come down to the dining room table.

The breakfast call wasn't coming. Finally, boots stomped on the back porch. The back door opened and closed softly with a sound of low voices, but we couldn't make out the words. Heavy steps told us both of our parents were coming upstairs. She came to the door, but held no breakfast trays. Pa appeared unsmiling, looked into our eyes and said softly, "Lady died." Shock and silence hung. We stared at the ceiling.

In a husky voice he added, "Our Lady died in her sleep. I found her snuggled against the straw pile."
More silence. More staring.

Finally, second-oldest Velma stirred, turned her face to the wall whispering, "Lady died because we've been stuck in the house more than a week." Velma was the perceptive one.

Tears slid down our pox-marked cheeks, making them itch.

Ma cautioned. "Try not to scratch, you'll make scars."

We slid between the cozy flannel sheets to mourn the loss of our Lady---the driving force that brought Louis and Frieda together to create our family.

Whispers of a Blizzard

Into the mid 1920's, Lady had still known her way home. Minnesota winter mornings when snow drifts were too deep and steep for us to wade the 3/4 mile walk to school, Pa hitched Lady to the cutter, tucked us under cowhide robes and sent us off with eldest sister Helen holding the reins.

At the schoolhouse door, we wriggled from under the robes and skittered into the schoolhouse stomping snow off our boots in the bell-tower entryway. Helen tied the reins around the whip holder, patted Lady and said, "Go home, Lady." Lady went home. Later in the day, her horse sense could not be trusted to return to school to pick us up. Who knew where she might wander off in search of oats or four-footed playmates? When school dismissed we'd walk home with the west wind pushing us home before dark.

Then came the only day we were allowed to skip school because a beastly blizzard threatened.

I knelt between four-year-old Paul and seven-year-old Donna at an upstairs bedroom window delighted with our very own white fairyland.

In my six-year-old wonderment, I mused, "Things look more real under snow." Paul and Donna both nodded, not un-cupping chins resting in their hands.

With elbows on the broad windowsill, our eyes scanned the fluffy snow covering the lawn, windmill and outbuildings. Rows of evergreens in the windbreak in front of the grove of maples, oaks, and butternuts now seemed closer, shrouded in undisturbed glistening.

Donna whispered, "See how close the windbreak looks now." Silently, Paul's and my chins dipped in our hands. We looked. Discovering. Wondering.

Paul squeaked, "What're those humps on top of the sheep barn?" We girls looked, shrugged, looked some more.

The storm door of the back porch banged with a winter thud. Pa, with earflaps pulled down and wool cap covering his eye brows, stepped into the snow, his boots making deep tracks to the cistern pump beside the back porch. He knotted a long rope to the crook of the pump handle. We three turned worried eyes to each other and shivered with dread remembering the neighbor who had frozen to death when he lost his way from his corncrib to his house.

Pa leaned into swirling ground squalls and stumped to the barn dragging that long rope across the lawn and across the barnyard to the hitching post outside the barn door. He looped the rope into a horseman's knot and gave it an extra tug.

Donna whispered, "Now he won't get lost when the blizzard comes." Paul and I nodded with relief.

Paul bragged. "Bet our Lady coulda found her way home in this blizzard."

As Big as a Squirrel's Ear

Rites of spring sprung as sure as the first crocus popped up and the day Pa stood in the kitchen and pronounced, "Leaves on the trees are as big as a squirrel's ear!" We knew this meant the ground was warm enough to plant corn.

Oh Boy! Our collective eyes turned to Ma pleading, "Can we take off our shoes and stockings today?"

With a knowing smile she nodded, "When the late morning sun shines on the living room east window for one solid hour you may go barefoot."

We huddled around that spot of sun on the floor at the east window waiting for the sun to beat the clock and free us from those dreadful lisle stockings and shoes. With or without shoes, Paul never had stood on ceremony. There's an early morning picture somewhere of him about nine years old, on his way to bring in the cows, bundled in his sheepskin coat, cap with ear flaps down. He's barefoot. And, no mittens. He was forever losing mittens and gloves, sending him through winter after winter with chapped hands and wrists.

On our way to school on early spring days, we couldn't wait for it to be dry enough to shed overshoes. We waited until we were out of sight to roll down our lisle stockings--held up by garters made of pieces of elastic---and push up the legs of our long cotton underwear. On the way home, hiding in wild berry bushes near our gate we re-folded our underwear at the ankles and smoothed stockings in place. By Friday our legs were grotesquely lumpy under the strain of an entire week's clandestine folding and stretching. Most of those shoes, overshoes and stockings kicked off in spring became hand-me-downs by fall.

Hand-Me-Down Clothes

The sight of spring's first serious thaw, or when autumn's first snowflakes stuck to the ground, we headed for the attic where Ma would already be up to her biceps in storage boxes. Lifting a sun suit, skirt, coat or snowsuit declaring, "This is still perfectly good," while her eyes took measure of which of us would fit into it. Claiming the garments assigned to us was as jolly as opening Christmas presents.

Oh happy day, that summer Sunday morning that we were called to the master bedroom. We were impressed to see *our* mother gussied up in a flouncy voile dress as she handed each of us our first anklets (later called bobby sox). Mine had purple flowers and lace edging. In church we admired our fancy feet holding them straight out, turning them this way and that, until her "all-seeing" hands reached over to squeeze our knees--her eyes never leaving the altar or pulpit. Our new anklets really *did* look dandy with our black patent leather shoes, which we had oiled during Saturday's chores.

Dressing alike for Helen and Velma ended as teenagers when they attended St. John's Lutheran parochial school in Wykoff where Professor Wallman decided Helen should skip a grade.

With part time jobs, they earned enough money to by an expensive coral wool dress they just *had* to have, so each paid half. It took some doing for Velma not to show up wearing that dress when dating one of Helen's hand-me-down boy friends.

To this day we cart or ship clothes across state lines, to the next township, or just next door to swap with each other, with our children, grandchildren and great-grandchildren--some of the styles back in fashion. Sister Donna, on her 79th birthday, visited my home in Malibu and "shopped" in my clothes closet for her birthday gifts that were "still perfectly good." Our mother would be proud.

Second youngest Marilyn strutted like a peacock in her very first dress that was *not* a hand-me-down. It was made of a 100 lb. flour sack with Gold Medal bleached out and trimmed with a red peter pan collar. When five-year-old Lois fell heir to a favorite coat she quietly grumbled to a friend after church about her coat sleeves being too short. Jovial Uncle George overheard her. He grinned. "That coat is very pretty on you, remember not to put your arms through all the way." It worked. Lois enjoyed her pretty coat, slightly hunching up her shoulders all winter.

Lilas, left. Lois in her too-short sleeves

Right here, Uncle George deserves a time out. He was full of fun anywhere, anytime. One Sunday he and Aunt Fern invited us and Pastor Deye to dinner. We circled dining room chairs to join the chatter in the living room until we heard, "Dinner's ready, bring your chairs to the table." Aunt Fern burst into laughter, nearly dropping the platter of roast pork, when she saw Uncle George and Pastor Deye at the table seated on the divan.

Memories of Uncle George's smiles that calmed fears and dried tears by cupping my face in his hands, fill me still with peace. He left a trail of peace and laughter. His many great grand-nephews and nieces could write a book about Uncle George.

Decades later my daughter, Jane, remembers with a smile. "When I was three, Uncle George convinced me I was grownup enough to help him wait on customers in his store. That same day he let three-year-old-cousin, Christy, and me climb on his lap to comb and style his hair with gooey stuff."

Bloody Noses

One early spring day after school, Paul hung back to horse around with the boys. He fell out of a tree and broke his nose. Donna, Lilas and I had not seen him fall. We were well on the way home with me boasting that Miss Kretzchmar had asked me to speak a piece in the Township's declamatory contest. The piece was about a bloody nose.

It happened that same afternoon, the Ladies Aid was meeting in our home. Remembering this put us in high gear to be home in time for store-bought buns and lunch meat sandwiches and sweet leftovers from their meeting.

Paul walked home alone. He realized the house was full of church ladies and veered off to the barnyard. He was in no mood to face a dozen or so ladies who would be ready to give advice and sympathy. He hung over the edge of the livestock watering tank to wash the blood off his face in icy water.

After the ladies left, Ma asked, "Did Paul get some treats?" We girls shrugged, changed out of school clothes and set the table while dinner cooked. Darkness came. The men came in for supper. Subdued light from a gas lamp hanging above the dinner table let Paul keep his face turned away from Ma, eat supper and slip off to bed. Lucky for him, by the time anyone noticed anything more than his usual bruises, his fresh cuts must have sealed with his own serum—God's handy glue—letting Paul pull off his charade.

I saved face in a couple of weeks by winning first prize in the humorous division in that declamatory competition. This happened the very day baby Meredith, daughter number nine was born. I don't remember the name of the 8- or 10-minute piece I presented in a German dialect. It told of a woman ranting about spending all day scrubbing floors ending with her complaining that her son had come home with a bloody nose "and all over my floor his nose goes." Laughter and applause rewarded me for the hours of the after school rehearsals.

Squeezing my eyes with the thrill of winning, I ran home to the birthing bed to show off my maroon award— breathlessly slipping in that Frank, my heart throb wearing a maroon waffle weave sweater, had won first in the oratorical division. Running out of puffed-up steam, it hit me that the world didn't really revolve around me. I peeked into the baby buggy to admire our newest and last baby sister, Meredith.

Paul's broken nose healed without incident, until World War II broke out. Paul's deviated septum was discovered by military doctors when he enlisted in the United States Merchant Marine. This didn't keep Lieutenant JG Paul H. Gehrke, Purser Pharmacist's Mate from crossing the equator seven times in defense of our country.

Lieutenant JG Paul H. Gehrke

Material Witnesses

Helen and Velma, the two oldest, a year apart in age, started first grade on the same day, took piano lessons together and usually dressed alike. Well ordered lives it seemed---until a commotion stirred the day Heinie Simpson, the rural-route mailman, delivered their first ready-made dresses from Montgomery Ward. Our favorite sight each day had been Heinie's big touring sedan pull up to our mailbox with his left-pointer finger giving us his tip-of-the-hat wave.

Seeing that package atop the mailbox sent all of us racing to hurry the package back up to the dining room table where Helen and Velma reverently tore at strings and wrappers. We little ones gawked and giggled. They held the dresses against themselves, then shot into the bedroom to try them on, re-appearing for a fashion show. Giggling turned to oohing and aahing as we smoothed our hands across the fabric. These store-bought dresses with yellow and brown diamond-shaped designs and puffed sleeves dominated our conversation for days.

After each of us settled on the picture of our choice, fabric from store-bought bolts was flung across the dining room table---already extended with extra leaves to accommodate our ever expanding family, including Grandpa G. plus a hired man and sometimes a hired girl.

Often fabric came from pieces of men's old suits with seams ripped with a razor blade, washed and hung to dry on the clothesline. Wielding those razor blades and avoiding unintended manicures or leaving spots of blood on the fabric was our least favorite chore. Reusable sections of the men's Sunday suits materialized into girls' skirts, jumpers, jerkins and coats. I was thrilled to have the luxury of choosing a color other than brown or black for my coat lining. I had no clue where that stray piece of recycled red material came from and didn't care. O happy breezes that made my coat flap open with a red flash for the world to see.

One by one we were called in for measuring and fittings during which I usually heard, "Stand still, don't be such a flibbertygibbet." She let us choose —"what kind of buttons would you like? how about a bit of trim? piping? bias tape? smocking? lace?" She could even tat the lace.

That New Home sewing machine was moved away from the wall so we could circle to watch her hands guide the fabric under the jumping-bean action of the needle, barely missing her fingers, as her feet rocked at break-neck speed on the treadle. No wonder she had trim ankles.

The magic of her nimble hands turning and twisting the fabric until a finished garment materialized mesmerized us as we subliminally absorbed impromptu lessons on how to sew bust darts, tucks, hems, gussets, edge stitching to the under, bound button holes...

She repeated over and over and then again for good measure her mantra, "sleeve right, dress wrong, sleeve right, dress wrong," which we soon mumbled in whispers or a sing-song each time one of us tackled sewing a dress, blouse or jacket. If one attempts to put sleeves in a garment without remembering "sleeve right, dress wrong" be prepared to hear "Girl, girl, even as you sew, so shall you rip."

Forty some years later my daughter, Jane, tells of the nervous fun she had with Grandma G. at the sewing machine. "When I was seven years old Grandma's calm patience made each step seem simple beginning with threading the needle, filling and replacing the bobbin, how to stitch a straight line and on how to turn corners. Grandma cautioned, ' Be sure to keep your fingers away from the needle, it's dangerous---you might break the needle and they're expensive'." Jane still giggles that breaking the needle sounded more serious than a broken finger.

Reminiscing on how these lessons materialized into Helen and Velma designing and sewing their own wedding gowns has kept our family in stitches as we celebrated their 90th birthdays in 2008-09.

Measuring Up

As soon as I was out of infant dresses after Christmas 1924, Donna, my older sister (by 13 months), and I dressed alike—same pattern, from the same bolt of fabric, each with distinguishing trims of our choice. Her black naturally curly hair, thick sweeping eyelashes and tiny stature decided what style we would wear. What a thrill the day when, at 4 and 5, we were allowed to tag along with the three big girls to visit school for a half day. We shared a desk and felt grown up taking turns dipping the pen into the ink well to write.

When it was time for Donna to enter first grade, my 10-lb birth weight had increased exponentially and my healthy crop of blonde buster-brown hair cut presented a solid, robust five-year-old who could fend for herself, would heave dainty Donna over Minnesota snow drifts and lift her to reach the cookie jar.

She went to first grade under protest. Every day she only cried at school. When asked why she didn't like school, she blubbered, "I don't like it because Anna isn't here."

"But she's not old enough to start school." The teacher and our parents explained.

"Then I'll wait until she gets old enough," sniffled Donna through wet lips pursed tightly to let them know she meant business.

Miss Perry and our parents didn't want to hold Donna back a year. They finally let me begin first grade with Donna. So it was, that I, at age 5, skipped a grade before ever starting school. Donna and I were confirmed in the same class and graduated from high school together.

In grade school, after we had mastered "The Little Red Hen" in our McGuffey Reader, Ma trusted us to read the recipe to stir up the batter for the family's favorite Cream Cake. She went to the cloak/wash room, put on her bonnet and went out to the garden, calling back, "Wash your hands first--- with soap."

We stood on chairs at the kitchen counter, the better to read the recipe, keep eggshells out of the bowl, measure dry ingredients and to take turns stirring with the wooden spoon. Donna handed me a coffee cup from our everyday set of china and sent me to the well house, roughly 200 feet from the kitchen, across the lawn and barnyard.

I dipped the cup into the cream can floating atop a plank in the tank of icy well water and shuffled back to the kitchen locking my eyes on the cream, willing it to stay in the cup. Not a drop spilled. Impressed with my steady hand, Donna stirred and sent me back for another cup of cream, then another and another.

Divine intervention must've led Ma to stop hoeing. She looked toward me asking, "How's your cake coming?"

"Fine," I bragged, not daring to look away from the wiggling cream. Shuffling on I added proudly, "only three more cups to go."

She dropped the hoe, vaulted two rows of blooming tomatoes and a patch   of cucumbers, swooped that fourth cup of cream from my hand, and flew into the kitchen, "Augh! It calls for only 3/4 cup." Too late. Donna was furiously stirring our soupy batter of cream. Duh!

We hadn't come to the pages on fractions in our arithmetic book, but had agreed that 3 and 4 equal 7. Shaking her head and making her tongue do meaningful tsk, tsks, Ma tried to hide her amusement while computing how many eggs and what proper portions of dry ingredients would resurrect our Cream Cake. With her enlarging family, she had the good sense to buy a cake pan holding a double recipe. That, and the regular-size cake pan with other acceptable cake-pan substitutes, saved our culinary effort. For two weeks no one asked, "What's for dessert?"

This three/fourths-seven episode was only one episode that prompted Pa to tag Donna and me as the Katzenjammer Kids. We laughed at Hans and Fritz when Grandpa G. read the Sunday funnies to us. Donna was labeled Fritz, I Hans.

Jens the Scarecrow

Jens was our scarecrow in the cornfield on the East 80 on our farm in Jordan Township, Minnesota. It was spring 1928. I remember because in March I had gotten to choose the flavor of homemade ice cream and lick the dasher for my 5th birthday. Each spring we put new clothes on Jens after going to the straw pile to pull out clean straw from the middle of the stack to plump up Jens.

He seemed never to get tired of waving his arms wearing Grandpa's last year's faded overalls and plaid mackinaw. Funny thing is his arms seemed to wave early in the morning and until late at night even without a wind. He waved at the horses pulling the hay wagons, the seeders and the harrows. Sometimes a car drove by for him to wave at, too. If that driver happened to be our silly cousin Melvin, he'd wave back at Jens. Melvin was a big tease.

Anyway, this day happened to be the day after the men had planted corn because last week, Pa had come into the kitchen and said, "Oak leaves are as big as a squirrel's ear. Time to plant corn." Good news for us kids. If the soil was warm enough to plant corn, we could go barefoot.

Mrs. Greenlee, across that cornfield where Jens lived, had just had a new baby boy; so, Donna, who was 6, and I, were sent to take over a batch of cookies and a pan of cinnamon rolls that were still hot. Carefully, we put our bare feet between the rows of newly seeded corn, but all of a sudden a bunch of squawking birds threw both of us off balance.

A crow was swooping down on Jens and trying to pick at his straw, but two sparrows kept chasing off the crow who sailed into the air. The sparrows looped around right after him. Not one of them would let up. We enjoyed their show until their wings slapped awfully close to our heads, making us put footprints on top of the planted rows.

Finally, we left the bird show and went on to Greenlees to deliver Ma's baked gifts before they cooled. We oohed and aahed at Mrs. Greenlee's sleeping baby. Mostly though, we couldn't wait to head home to tell the "big girls" about the bird show they'd missed.

I ran into our kitchen yelling, "You shoulda seen what we saw out by the sparecrow!"

SPAREcrow? older sister, Bee, wrinkled her nose and laughed sorta smart alecky. Oldest sister, Helen, smirked, "There's no such thing as a sparecrow."

I flinched and flounced off mumbling, "Well there *were* sparrows by the scarecrow. So there."

It was harder to get anything past my big sisters than it is to kiss my own elbow.

Chicken Feed

Having set my pace as an early riser, when that ob/gyn doctor had slapped my bottom at 4:32 a.m. in 1923, paid off in 1930 on an early summer morning when Pa had an errand to run in Stewartville, 12 miles from home.

"Yes," he nodded. "you may go along if you can be at the pickup in five minutes."

I ran to the kitchen, cracked an egg into the frying pan on the already hot cook stove, stabbed the spatula at it to spread the yolk, stood on my tiptoes to flip it, sawed off a slice of homemade bread, scooped the egg out of the pan and slid it onto the crooked piece of bread, scuttled along the brick walk across the lawn out to the Ford pickup parked outside the lawn gate. I clenched my breakfast between my teeth so I could use both hands to hoist myself onto the running board to open the pickup door.

I was in time. He was just coming out of the machine shed with a coil of rope and block and tackle which he flung into the back of the pickup.

I looked down at my everyday cotton dress with a questioning look for approval. He said it was okay because it was clean. The cracked leather seat made my thighs itch, but it felt cool through the thin cotton.

I didn't know why we were going to Stewartville and didn't care. It was enough to go along and none of those sleepyhead sisters and brother were getting to go. Besides I would have a window seat all to myself.

"Do you think you can you pull the choke while I crank?"

"Sure, I know how to do that," I bragged.

He cranked. The motor clattered to life and he climbed in at the steering wheel, pulled down the gas feed on the steering post and rolled out of the yard gate and turned west on the gravel road with the sun warming our backs.

Self-importance squelched my appetite. Isinglass window curtains had been folded and tucked above and behind the seat, letting me hang my face out the open window with the breeze mussing my buster-brown haircut.

"Please, God, let it look like I don't really have straight bangs at all and that the wind parts my hair to the side, just like the big girls," I muttered silently. I couldn't wait until my 10th birthday to have their hairstyles.

Soon the half-eaten egg was cold. It curled at the edges. I nibbled daintily to make it look as though I was eating. Wasting food was unthinkable, so I kept my mouth busy asking questions---not nice to talk with food in your mouth. "Who lives in that house? Is that where Perry Ellis lives? How many kids do they have?" We fairly well shouted over the noise of the pickup and the wind.

My mouth was dry. I squirmed and halfway chewed on the leathery egg. After a while we came upon a flock of chickens poking around in the ditch for their breakfast. Keeping his eyes on the road, Pa lifted his right forefinger from the steering wheel, pointed at the chickens and said, "Why not let those chickens eat the rest of your breakfast."

I shot a look at him that must have said, "Really?"

He nodded. The egg sailed out the window. The chickens fluttered and flocked around my offering like vultures. My mouth wasn't dry any more. I don't think I ever thanked him.

Whistling Girls and Crowing Hens

Word of a barn dance in Jordan Township, Minnesota in early summers of the 1920-30's with barns and hay lofts---now emptied of last year's crops and before the next harvest appeared---musicians appeared out of the woodwork to entertain entire families from at least three neighboring townships.

In Uncle Tader's barn a handsome favorite cousin, 19-year-old Elmer, danced with flair making a spectacle by swinging me, a third grader, so high I barely missed kicking the hips of other dancers. A more respectable spectacle was created by our parents. Their interpretation of the music sometimes cleared the floor as other dancers stood aside to admire them. He lifted her right hand high with lofty reverence. Years later, he proudly assumed this same mood as he handed each of his nine daughters down the aisle.

Romance never had it so good as when our parents glided to the sensations of "Good Night, Sweetheart." I wished these nights would never end.

Our parents had superior ears for music, with singing voices to match, passing along an early appreciation for music as each infant, in turn, lay with an ear against our mother's breast in church as she sang hymns, often Bach Chorales. She played our pump organ and Gulbrandson upright piano despite those two crippled fingers on her right hand permanently shaped into question marks by that runaway team crashing into their buggy when she was six months old.

He could come up with any tune you asked for on his harmonica. And, that man could whistle. His whistling "Now the Moon Shines Tonight on Pretty Red Wing..." wafting through the heating ducts as he fired up the furnace early winter mornings was a worthy substitute for summer's rooster's crow drifting through open windows.

It was easy to follow his continual whistling when it was time to bring water or mid-morning lunch to him in the fields. Whistling looked easy. I wanted to learn how.

One day I followed his whistle and found it mixed with the sound of the flat squared-off shovel scraping the cement manure gutters in the cow barn. Twinkle and Tuff, the dapple grey team hitched to the manure spreader in the alleyway between the milk-cow stanchions, patiently waited switching their tails at pesky horse flies while he scooped gutters.

I asked, "How do you whistle?"

"Nothing to it, just pucker up and blow." A line I later heard repeated by Lauren Bacall in the 1944 movie "To Have and Have Not," made me smile in the darkened theatre.

Puckering my lips went sort of okay. Blowing out was easy, but blowing in brought tears to my eyes from the acrid fumes of manure. After a few coughs, he laughed and sent me into the fresh air to try again. Finally, I tamed a few bars of "Old Dan Tucker."

The reward for not blowing that tune? He invited me to climb on the seat beside him and ride to the flax field on the back 40 to spread the load behind us. It was peculiar fun to watch the chains on the spreader bed move while the spiked iron wheels scattered fertilizer to produce food for the cattle, hogs and poultry that we would eventually eat to complete nature's food cycle---"just the way God intended it."--- our favorite retort when we couldn't come up with logical answers; such as the first time we saw the Volkswagen Bug car. We snorted, "That will never catch on with its engine in the back. Engines should be in front 'the way God intended it'." We had a lot to learn besides whistling.

In the flax field, he handed me the reins to turn Twinkle and Tuff toward the barn and I practiced whistling while he sang "Old Dan Tucker was a fine old man, washed his face in a frying pan, combed his hair with a wagon wheel, died with a toothpick in his heel."

Whistling gave me pleasure even though the sisters who never did learn to whistle chided, "Whistling girls and crowing hens come to a bad end."

Big Deal! I grew up to tell about it.

Grandma Krumdieck

Our chief priestess of sewing was Grandma K who each morning, when she reached for her eyeglasses her thimble was never far behind. These two pragmatic companions, along with the ever-ready straight pins and threaded needles poked into her bodice or the bib of her apron were daily accessories.

No split seam, sagging hem, or loose button (no matter that it might be on the shirt of one of our boyfriends calling for his date) got past her. Anyone's clothing anytime was fair game even though one dropped by just to say hi, to check on her health, or to visit her cookie jar. She reminded us to sit down to eat, even for only a cookie "because it's hard on your heart to eat standing up."

I had stopped by for a quick visit. With threaded needle poised in mid air, her slight frame closed in on my offending attire. I backed toward the door, "Later, Grandma, I'm running late." She faked a scowl and said, Stand still, girl, you can't go out looking like that. Where's your self-respect? It'll take just a minute." Within that minute, she stitched me up, bit off the thread, and sent me out to meet the world to step smartly, heady with self-respect.

One day, she clapped a hand over her mouth to hold in her laughter and dentures when she told of three-year-old Meredith (baby of our family) standing rigid as a mannequin for the fitting of her half-finished dress, still in the basted stage. Smoothing the fabric over Meredith's tiny body, Grandma asked, "There now, how do you like that?" Meredith held back tears, but forced a smile not to hurt Grandma's feelings, "It's nice, but I'd like it better if it had two sleeves." Grandma quickly gathered up Meredith with the promise, "It will have two sleeves when it's finished."

Every Second Christmas Day and occasional Sunday dinners at Grandma's table, covered with white linen stretched to accommodate 14 people, were always an *event.* When I was tall enough to sit on a grownup chair without a Montgomery Ward catalog to see over my plate, Grandma served my wine in an elegant glass scarcely larger than her thimble. Admiring the glass and savoring the wine, I could hardly stand the thrill of my grownup status. Through the years at the communion rail her silver thimble flashes to mind.

Following Grandpa K.'s death, Grandma lived with us in St. Paul. We set her up in the den with her sewing machine, but not for long. Convinced that she was missing out on the comings and goings coming from our bedroom directly above the den, she suggested her bed be moved up with the other two double beds, sleeping three each. A good time was had by all, until from the master bedroom across the hall we heard, "Hire a hall!" Silence and snoring reigned.

Television sets began showing up in private homes in the 1940's. Grandma K's fascination with this moving-picture-in-a-box contraption had her pull up her chair and paste her face to the screen. One afternoon, no one had the heart to tell her they could now see only a corner of the screen. She wasn't about to miss her granddaughter riding as a princess on the "Queen of Hearts" float sponsored by Schmidt's Brewery. Two nights later--- after Grandma's bedtime---the rest of the family got their glimpse of me waving to the crowds in frigid February in the annual Winter Carnival's Torchlight Parade.

Surrounded by seamstresses, oddly, crocheting never caught on with us beyond simple doilies and napkin rings. During one visit, jolly Great Aunt Sophie taught several of us to knit. Teaching me how to wind the hank of yarn into a ball and how to hold the knitting needles, she guided my fingers to cast the yarn onto the needles. With lots of giggling, she started me on a trivet for hot dishes. That went well, so it was on to a pair of bedroom socks for my father's Christmas present. The more I knit, the less it looked like a sock, but he pulled it on his foot for a trial.

The family pointed and laughed. What a waste of yarn. Someone suggested it might make a good hat. I pulled it on my head. More pointing and laughing. It was perfect as an army garrison-like hat. It kept my head warm several winters. He never did get his bedroom socks, but several people did ask where I'd bought the smart garrison cap.

Our mother, that woman with clever crooked fingers and exceptional creativity, had never learned to knit. Years later, now a grandmother, she wanted to make an afghan, so we got her started with fiendish relish, each day inspecting her work. "Slipped a stitch. Do it over. Too lumpy. Unravel. Redo." Sweet revenge for the rip-and-redo supervision she had schooled us on. Once she got the hang of knitting, afghans draped everywhere ready for stray chills.

Krumdieck cousins LaVern, Erma, Carl
and Walter . Elmer on Grandma's lap.
Grandpa holding me, Helen,
Bee, Velma and Donna

Joy Riding with the Old Folks

Grandpa and Grandma had come from town to our farm for Sunday dinner and I was to go home with them. Their high, narrow car had skinny tires and two doors, one on each side, in the middle of the car. From the running board one stepped onto the floor of the back seat, edged between the two front seats, turned right if you were a passenger, left if you were the driver. Grandma, at barely five feet, boarded with finesse and draped her crazy-quilt lap robe over her knees. I, nine years old, climbed in the back seat.

Grandpa stood in front of the engine cranking while Grandma pulled the choke as he instructed. The motor sputtered, caught hold, and shimmied the car like a hen in a dust bath. He climbed in. I moved my legs aside to give his six-foot-two frame space to wedge between the front seats and to settle behind the wheel.

Grandma clutched the knob of her window crank with one hand and gripped the dashboard with the other. Grandpa lurched the car down the driveway through the yard gate. He turned east toward town, pulled the gas feed on the steering rod down to the maximum and for eight miles flogged those horses under the hood as though he held reins and a buggy whip rather than a steering wheel.

Our tracks rounded off the sharp turns at Crowson's stone quarry and gravel pit. He rattled down Niemeyer hill, cut-the-pie at Carson's corner, rumbled across Root River bridge into town, climbed Bendickson hill, turned left on Main Street, right on Church Street, wheeled into their driveway where he switched off the ignition—*not then, not for eight miles had he touched the brake*. Grandma said not a word. She long ago had accepted his Barney Oldfield's race-car driving philosophy. I accepted the power of prayer.

Elegy for Grandpa K.

Your left eye sparked as I strode up
the slope
to your side porch where at 4:30 each
day
you waited on the cracked leather
couch.
That patch on your right eye intrigued
me.
Your lips twitched with a twinkle ready
to tell
stories about that lost eye, some of
them true.

Once as Grandma and I stitched and
chatted,
you pretended to be asleep in your
recliner.
She dimpled, "Ach, he's asleep
already." I
said, "Of course, he has only one eye
to close."
Her hand held back her laughter and
dentures.
You lifted an eyebrow, your lips turned
up.

As official bell ringer, you counted it a
privilege to toll the church bell three
times
during the Lord's Prayer on Sundays
and at funerals.
One Easter, you lay abed a block
from church.
During Sunrise services on toll
number three
you drew your last breath at the "Amen."

Then you lay on satin in your living room
wearing the blue tie with white stripes,
my last gift on your 89th birthday.
Your bride of 63 years milled through
the crowd of mourners; she reached my
ear
and whispered, "He asked to wear your
tie."

The whole town, verily, the entire
county,
arranged to honor you at your funeral.
But, your funeral in the school
auditorium?
With no bell? How dare they? I was
wrong.
Vibrations of love and respect rang off
those walls,
echoing your "Amen" toll embracing you
in peace.

Grandpa Gehrke

Widower Grandpa G. charmed us by reading to us the comic strip "Dorothy Darnit" for our earliest reading lessons, in a perfect mixture of English and/or German. This got me in trouble with Miss Perry, our red-haired Irish lady, when I answered in German. Foolishly, I let myself be intimidated enough to lose my facility with German.

We knew lessons on telling time were coming when Grandpa's fingers squirmed into his watch pocket to pull out his gold watch on a chain and snap the lid open---his mustache twitching in a friendly smile. His patience in keeping us preschoolers occupied with cards launched us into learning our KQJ's before our ABC's for a lifetime of pinochle, whist, euchre, hearts, old maid, gin rummy, bridge, canasta, double solitaire....

Herding sheep beside him in the pasture gave deeper meaning to shepherd stories and memory verses from Sunday School while we made a game of choosing names for gamboling lambs that pounced like puppets, annoying the ewes.

Hanging over the top of the bottom half of the Dutch door on the sheep barn at sheep shearing time and watching men clip, clip,clipping to peel rolls of wool from a wiggling, bleating (or bleeding from an occasional nick) was only half the fun. Next we'd get into a frenzy jostling to unlatch the door before a just shorn sheep tried to butt the door open trying to escape the embarrassment of its nudity. Then slamming the door shut to keep those still wooly sheep inside was tricky fun. Grandpa took over door duty when it was the sheep buck's turn to be wrestled under those hand clippers. With flaring nostrils, he lunged against his collar and rope-the buck, not Grandpa.

Three-year-old Lilas's morning chore was to wake Grandpa for breakfast. Her earliest memory is the day she went to his room, climbed on his bed to wake him; but, this day she ran downstairs in tears, "Grandpa won't wake up." Within the hour, a knock came on the schoolhouse door. Miss Perry answered and stepped into the entryway beneath the bell tower for hushed words with our father who was granted permission to gather his children to take us home.

All too soon I had an almost surreal glimpse of our mother as I happened past the washroom to see her resting her forehead on the window, tears streaming down her cheeks. The undertakers were carrying Grandpa's body across the side lawn to the hearse. It was the first time I saw our mother cry.

For funerals in the 1920's and 30's, undertakers returned the embalmed body to the family's parlor until the day of the funeral. We experienced this very custom with equanimity when Grandpa G. died. When our father was only two years old, his mother Grandma Anna, nee Stender Gehrke, died giving birth to a daughter,

Anna, my namesake, who died within months.

For me, the sedateness of funerals intensified the dignity of the deceased, at the same time coalescing my wonderful world of great aunts' perfumes and great uncles' cigar aromas. Funerals let us become acquainted with second or third cousins whom we saw less often than first cousins.

One day, at Great Aunt Dora's farm house for a reception following a cemetery service, my eyes feasted on a table loaded with food fit for Sunday dinners. Rather than filling my plate I stared at the bustle of relatives swirling past my eyes at yard-stick height. I slipped into the pantry for solitude to take in the delicious day and comforting aromas, remembering Grandpa G's pipe.

Saturday Baths

The beauty of our plumbing was never calling a plumber for clogged sinks, tub drains or toilets in the 1920's and 30's on our Minnesota farm.

Plumbing was confined to outdoors piping water from the windmill to the livestock's drinking tank. Indoor plumbing came under the heading of outhouse, toilet, restroom, little girls' room, little boys' room, or bathroom--we called it the back house. At the propitious time, the men dug and shoveled dirt to make a deep hole of proper dimensions. They hitched a horse to a sturdy rope bound around the back house. With a slap on the horse's rump the men steered the horse to drag and reseat the back house over its new site.

The newly dug dirt was shoveled back to cover the former site as a compost pile. Recycling for us was already in vogue. Toilet paper was last season's Sears and Roebuck or

Montgomery Ward catalog pages vigorously crumpled into pulp.

Actually, there *was* a bathroom in the house, but no running water or plumbing. We did have a proper oblong bath tub.

Saturdays we pumped and carried water from the cistern just off the back porch for baths and shampoos. A shampoo in soft rainwater is pure opulence, giving us shiny crowns of glory. Hauling and heating water in a boiler on top of the cook stove and in the reservoir attached to the end of the cook stove took longer than bathing itself. Sheer luxury was to be one of the first batch in the tub; and sheer heaven to eventually be old enough to sit in the tub alone. Even though teakettles of fresh hot water were added after each bather, it wasn't the same as being first.

In the grip of Minnesota winters, the tub was brought into the kitchen in front of the open hot oven door of the blazing wood stove. A cozy treat. One Saturday I announced, "I am big enough to dry myself." Loath to trust this uppity tot, Mother handed me a towel, "All right, but move away from the stove."

I took the towel and promptly sat on the oven door to dry my feet. I screamed. Somebody scooped me up, and plopped me bottom first into the nearest snow bank. So much for being "big enough." Being "too big for my britches" was more like it. Scars? None. Take my word for it.

Ten-month-old Velma on the side lawn
of the old house. Note the bathtub
hanging near the back door

Pets and Fall Cleaning

Following Saturday baths in winter, the warm oven sometimes became a nursery for frail newborn lambs bedded down in the kitchen. We took turns bottle feeding and playing nurse to our woolly toys, but were not allowed to turn them into house pets. We waited for turns to bottle feed newborn calves, but only in their barn stalls.

I don't remember that bathroom being used for much other than warm weather Saturday night baths, a place to wash home-brew bottles with soapy water and buckshot, for storing home brew, or for storing the shotgun nailed next to the ceiling over the door. Being allowed to sip foam from a glass of home brew made washing bottles worth the effort.

That shotgun came down from its hook to kill 30 hogs the day they escaped from their pen and picked up cholera from another herd. Rumor has it too much home brew played a part in lack of keeping an eye on the stray hogs. True or not, back-breaking hole digging to bury these lost porky profits dug even deeper in our already sagging economy.

Years earlier, that shotgun had come off the bathroom wall on the day our black and white sheep dog, Mupsy, turned sheep killer. Poor blood-thirsty Mupsy had to go. He was replaced by Perk, a caramel and white Terrier, who came perilously close to getting the shotgun treatment for pulling laundry off the clothesline. His even greater sin was the dawn he broke into the back porch to raid our individual Easter baskets. Our parents found him out in time to quickly boil and color eggs for a community basket. Fragments of our individual baskets strewn about the lawn and barnyard showed up for days, peeving Ma at Perk all over again for the messes he'd made.

To her, "cleanliness is next to godliness" not only applied to Perk, but included us. We knew we were in for it when she broke into singing "Work for the Night is Coming." Straw and/or cornhusk ticks and feather beds flew out of the upstairs windows to be laundered or aired on the clotheslines for a session with the rug beater. Any girl showing signs of lagging behind during spring or fall cleaning was jarred with, "Beaus don't go where cobwebs grow."

Cleaning the one-room schoolhouse at District 98 the week before school started landed on our to-do list. True, Pa was secretary of the school board, but surely cleaning the school didn't fall to the secretary's wife and family; though we did pretty well outnumber the number of students from other families. Lucky for us, though, as school board member, he had a hand in hiring our favorite teacher, Miss Kretzchmar, who also happened to be our pastor's daughter.

Whatever the reason for us cleaning the schoolhouse, we supposed it had something to do with the oft-heard, "If it needs doing, quit talking about it and DO it." We hauled water loaded on the same little wagon we used for hauling firewood and traipsed the 3/4 mile to District 98. All horses were busy in the harvest fields, so we carried bundles of cleaning rags, a broom, mop, bars of Fels Naptha soap and scrub brushes to spend the entire day shining up the schoolhouse with a break for a picnic lunch on the lawn. Meredith was too small to help, so Marilyn got to play with her outside.

No goofing off for them years later during Saturday cleanings after we moved to St. Paul. We big girls mopped and dusted the downstairs rooms and the master bedroom keeping time to and singing along with Texaco Hour's Metropolitan Opera broadcasts. Marilyn and Meredith cleaned our bedroom upstairs while listening to the "Let's Pretend" radio program, all the while squabbling about who was doing the most work. As adults, Marilyn said that Meredith admits to being the better shirker. Must be tough to be the baby of the family.

Back to School

Excitement built around dog days of late August as we looked forward to going to Chatfield's corner Five 'n Dime to choose our new tablets or replenish our pencils, pens and boxes of crayons. From there we headed a few doors down Main Street to buy school shoes. In Oscar Fahlgren's Shoes we sat on a long bench to have our feet measured. Mr. Fahlgren sized up what was needed, asking what kind of shoes we'd like. His climbing up the extension ladder that moved back and forth on rollers had us wide eyed and envious. Oh, how we wished we were allowed to climb the windmill ladder at home. He'd bring down our shoe selections from the floor-to-ceiling stacks of boxes. Decisions and comparisons were kept to a whisper---after all we were in public.

Another day Ma drove Donna, Paul, and me in the Cadillac into town to shop. She assigned a package to each of us to carry. A mile out of town, to my chagrin she discovered my package wasn't in the car. She pulled the Cadillac to the side of the gravel road to make a U-turn and slid into the ditch.

I got to hike back a couple hundred yards to ask Claude Ferguson for a horse to pull us out. We drove back to town and sure enough my package was on the store counter just where I had left it. Boy oh boy, was she disgusted with me---so was I.

Our moods changed a few days later on the way home from Sunday morning services near that same spot of the sliding-in-the-ditch episode. As we crossed the Root River Bridge, Pa announced, "Summer is over." He tossed his stiff-brimmed straw hat out the car window sailing it down the river. Ma grinned and we children gasped at his marvelous extravagance.

Within a few days, it was back to school, back to carrying water. There was no well on the school grounds. During lunch hour students took turns in pairs to haul drinking water from Anderson's, about 1/4 mile west.

After trying not to slosh water on each other, the leftover water was poured into a fountain in the wood box room beside the stove at the back of the schoolroom.

That stove wore a protective jacket over its inferno innards to warm us and our lunches. Each winter morning, the teacher stood on a chair to reach over the stove's jacket to place the lunches of soup, goulash in mason jars, onto a platform built by some of the fathers. Hers was a precarious daily routine each morning and again at noon handing down the hot lunches as she teetered on a chair. Teachers dressed up in their best with stockings and dress shoes—no slacks or running shoes for stability that could have made this lunch routine safer.

Pumped Up

Washing clothes on Monday and ironing on Tuesday never varied---snow, sun or sleet; unless, the neighbors had a new baby or their mother was sick. Monday or not, we'd be sent to pick up the neighbors' laundry.

Pumping water from the cistern just outside the back door put washday in high gear.

Speaking of gear reminds me of feeling grown up when I was tall enough to pull the windmill in gear to keep the livestock tank filled or for the well-house tank (where the cream and butter were kept cold). I still feel that pumped up surge the first time I managed to prime the cistern pump.

A dry summer leaving the cistern empty, forced us back to pumping to carry water for baths and laundry from the windmill 100 feet or so from the back door. It took several trips of two of us to a pail to fill the boiler on top of the cook stove in which the clothes were boiled. Ma, or a tall girl, was allowed to lift out the steaming clothes with a heavy wooden stick rounded to keep from fraying the clothes. The hot, dripping clothes were lifted into the dishpan for transfer to the washtubs set up outside in good weather.

Bending over a scrub board rubbing a bar of homemade soap (in good times, she bought Fels Naphtha to go after stubborn stains) on the clothes in steaming water grazed the armpits building muscles, sore knuckles and backaches. Shorter scrubbers got off without backaches as they could scarcely see the business end of the scrub board let alone bend over the tub.

Until we got a hand-cranked wringer clamped between the tubs, we wrung each piece by hand. Two more tubs held the rinse water, one warm the other cold and we'd swing the wringer from one tub to the next to squeeze out the most possible water. For each load of white clothes bluing was added to the rinse water.

In winter, laundry took place in the basement, sometimes stringing lines down there to dry the clothes. Thank God there was a drain so we didn't have to carry the water upstairs. Unless there was a blizzard or below zero temperatures, clothes hung outside to freeze dry. I expected these stiff-as-board items would break when removing the clothespins, but they never did. Sweet smelling sheets, towels, petticoats, underpants. made inhaling sheer luxury.

When not using bar soap, ingredients for home-made soap bubbled in a cauldron over an open fire down by the smoke house. Years later, Helen and Lois could still whip up a batch of homemade soap; I never got the hang of it beyond knowing it called for lye.

Freeze drying clothes worked, but wash and wear hadn't been invented yet, so it was back to that trusty cook stove to heat flat irons picked up with clip-on handles. All shirts, many blouses and dresses were starched with powder starch dissolved in water. Dampening the clothes with a sprinkler head on a bottle and rolling the clothes into sausages was Monday night's ritual for Tuesday's ironing. Ironing boards on collapsible legs were not readily available, so our board was laid across the end of the dining room table and the back of a chair—-what a nuisance to have to lift the end of the board to insert the board into a skirt, dress or sleeve. Later we had separate sleeve boards.

Pumping and carrying drinking water from the windmill fell to the men until two of us grew tall enough to tote the pail without splashing water on each other. The pail of drinking water, with a community dipper, stood at the end of the cloakroom/washroom sink. The sink, with no drain, was a large pan of water for washing hands and faces---neck and ears, too, in case Ma was looking.

We felt privileged when pipes were laid from the windmill to a hand pump at the the washroom sink with a drain. No more bickering and tongue lashing about who's turn it is to carry out and dump that large pan of water.

Each winter many a tongue of gullible   disbelievers lost skin to cold pump handles or strips of metal. Testing this tongue theory on early morning frost on bedroom windows got us a sound scolding and a job of washing the window.

Squirreling Away for Winter

Canning season brought more pumping and carrying water on our farm in the 1920's. Forth and back, forth and back from the cistern and windmill to fill the boiler on our black range in the kitchen. Water boiled for scrubbing and scalding mason jars and lids for the 500 quarts of vegetables and fruits plus several dozen jam and jelly jars. Add to that two-quart jars for dill pickles, which I got to wash every year because I fell for "your hands fit into the jars perfectly."

I had failed to heed oldest sister Helen's warning, "Don't be too good at a job, or you get stuck with it." She spoke from experience, having been stuck with weeding because she was the only one who knew a weed from young sprouts of dill and ground cherries. Ground cherries became my downfall when it was noticed I was the only one trusted to pick them without eating them. Couldn't stand what seemed to me bland balls of gelatin stuffed into tiny Japanese lantern skins.

Our water brigade went into action again to fill the boiler to cook those 500 mason jars we had filled with sweet corn that we cut off the cob, shelled peas, strung and sliced string beans and wax beans, peeled and sliced beets---not to mention the jars of stew meat canned during butchering season.

A wooden rack was built to hold the jars a bit above the bottom of the boiler to keep a jar of vegetables or meat from exploding. Though, a couple of times an explosion did put a shot of zest into the drudgery of canning. It's a miracle Ma didn't burn herself or smash jars as she hoisted them out of the scalding water. After the jars were sealed and cooled, we carried them to the basement, lining them in pretty rows on the shelves, then standing back to admire the fruit of our labors.

As soon as overnight temperatures fell to freezing, slaughtering of hogs and beef called for gallons of scalding water to scrape the stiff, wiry hair off the carcasses before halving/quartering them to be hung on hooks in the machine shed.

More scalding water was needed to scrub the wooden dining room table, turning it into the butcher board. One by one, the men brought quarters and halves of pork or beef in from the machine shed to be carved into chops, hams, slabs of bacon, T-bones, spare ribs, loins, roasts...whatever our Chef Frieda had ordered.

She, Pa and Freddie Baier, the bachelor butcher down the road, wielded cleavers and carving knives until it was time to clamp the meat grinder to the table, slip the casings from the butcher shop or previously boiled intestines on to the grinder nozzle, crank the handle and voila!– sausages. Sausages hung with hams, slabs of bacon, ribs, etc. in the smoke house where a smoldering fire did its work sending up aromas to try the soul of the most dedicated vegetarian. Non-smoked meat was seasoned, wrapped and laid out on the glazed front porch facing north---a forerunner of no-defrost refrigerators.

Our menu varied when Ma stalked the yard for geese and ducks or invaded the chicken coop. Squawking and fluttering feathers fazed her not a bit– she had the fastest hands in the Midwest. Before any bird could cry foul, his neck was on the chopping block, plunged into scalding water, stripped of pin feathers,"de-inarded" and headed for the oven.

We dug potatoes and pulled root vegetables for the men to load into the truck which they backed across the lawn, removed a basement window and ran a chute down to unload into the wooden potato bin. A smaller bin was filled with sand to store carrots, rutabagas, winter radish, horseradish, turnips, and some of the hardier brands of apples. On winter evenings, best manners called for one or two of us girls to bring apples up from the basement to be washed, placed in the cut glass bowl and passed around to company.

Our nostrils twitched the day washed and pared apples embellished with spices (notably cinnamon) were mixed in an enamel dishpan for apple butter and put in the oven. As soon as this bubbled, the oven door was set ajar to temper the heat. Our eyes and noses gravitated to the kitchen on imagined errands to watch the fragrant apple butter erupt with amusing squirts for hours until it was judged the right consistency to be transferred into mason jars or stored in gallon stone crocks.

Once we tried to raise popcorn. Meredith, remembers it was a trial to shuck that stuff and was glad we didn't give popcorn another go. Less work, though a bit dicey, was building a quick hot fire with kerosene-soaked corncobs for popping corn. Pa took charge with, "Stand back" as he set a match to the corncobs. After the conflagration settled down, popcorn was put in the pan, covered and shuffled until popping enough batches to roll popcorn balls in syrup ready for feasting.

We went to the cabbage patch with knives to cut off heads of cabbage to be carried to the basement for sauerkraut. Here Pa sat and straddled a 30-gallon stone crock with the kraut cutter across the top to slide back and forth, back and forth until every cabbage head was shredded. Salt, or whatever else went into this delicacy, became part of our standard Sunday dinners in winter. We gathered around to be entertained by this annual sauerkraut-cutting in the basement. Let Minnesota's winter come; our larder was stocked to the gills.

Thanksgiving Day after my third birthday, we rode home from church in the sleigh, bed blankets on top of us, horse blankets on a bed of straw under us. Pa, in his sheepskin floor-length overcoat with his collar covering all but his eyes and nose, with cap flaps pulled over his ears, stood at the front holding the reins. He worked his chin out to unmuffle his mouth and called. "What's in the oven for dinner?"

"Pork chops and sauerkraut," came the answer.

I objected, "But it's not Sunday, we can't have sauerkraut." The big girls laughed. I was embarrassed.

He winked at me, "There's no law says we can't have sauerkraut even if it's not Sunday."

I made a "so there" face at the big girls.

Squirreling Away
Photo courtesy of Joyce Haack

High Finance and Dancing

A $20 bill (a rare sight even for grownups) in my hands at age 10 was almost too much to bear. Our parents had to be away and trusted me to pay the man when he delivered the coal. This load would be shoveled down the chute through a window of the basement furnace room. Taking what seemed like a stance of authority near the truck until it was unloaded, and making sure the little kids were at the dining room window to watch, I waited for my moment to deal in high finance. Grandly handing over the $20 bill to the man when he said "thank you" I was primed and ready to smile and use the phrase, "much obliged" just as I had heard grownups say.

Coal was shoveled into that same basement furnace room in which the men braced a telephone pole to brace the dining room floor above. Promise of a house dance party was in the air when we spotted the men cart that pole down the outside trap door in preparation of merriment. Exhilaration escalated throughout the house as two or three of us fell to our knees around the bottom shelf of the library table that held our prize potted fern and a Christmas cactus along with the Bible.

In our best Palmer Method penmanship we made perfectly formed sweeping strokes on penny post cards, and wrote: "You are cordially invited to a dance at Gehrkes on Friday, ___ 15, 19_ at 7 p.m. Please bring sandwiches." Some were asked to bring pickles, some cake, some Jello, etc. to round out midnight supper. On the day of the dance our upright Gulbransen piano reigned supreme in the archway between the dining room and living room after all furniture, including the revered pump organ, had been stacked on the front porch.

Our family's best friend and neighbor, Isabelle, a master of any keyboard, played any tune at the exact tempo the dancers could keep up with. Violin virtuosos, the Baier boys from down the road, completed the never-die combo taking time out only to re-tune their instruments and down a slug of home brew.

All ages took to the dance floor, including babes rocking between their swaying parents until their tiny eyelids sank into repose. Babies were bedded down nearby for us to keep an eye on them. Everyone danced the fox trot, two step, and waltz; except me. I hung back until the musicians played a schottish since I never got the hang of flowing in sync with my partner. However, fifty-four years later one day *The Wizard of Oz's* Straw Man, Ray Bolger, bowed, offered his hand and propelled me around the Bel-Air CC golf shop molding me into amazing grace itself. Is it possible all those years it was not I who didn't have the knack of following, but those partners who didn't have the knack of leading? Nah.

Thunder and Spuds

Minnesota's severe electrical storms and thunder shivered our timbers until we scrambled out of bed and scampered down to the front porch where our parents had already slammed shut the windows. That heavy rain seemed not to be able to find its own path down the drenched windows. Here we sat out heaven's fracases. The flashier and louder the cracks of lightning and thunder the louder we sang, "Old Dan Tucker" along with "Oh the Moon Shines tonight on my Pretty Redwing." "The Red River Valley"... or we'd take turns picking a favorite hymn. I chose "Little Brown Church in the Vale" because I liked the lilt in the line about the wildwood.

Eleanor, the hired girl, told us thunder was God beating rugs for His spring cleaning. She also told us when you drop a fork on the floor it meant company (a woman) was coming, a knife meant a man and a spoon meant we should expect a child at the door. The company would come from the direction the utensil was pointing. Her tales were a bit hard to swallow.

So, when it came to understanding thunder, I stuck with Miss Kretzchmar's version in science class; thunder was God announcing that lightning was coming lickety split to put nitrogen into the soil for good crops. I don't remember that she also said that lightning gave shots of potassium or carotene to the soil; I do know we got to do our part at planting potatoes when "It's time to plant spuds!," rang out.

The men ploughed, disked and dragged a patch for potatoes smack dab in line with their going and coming from the fields each day. This ingenious plan, suggested by Ma, got rid of weeds between rows each time the men lowered the plow shares as they chose a different row in the garden morning and evening going and coming from the fields. Too bad it didn't get rid of pesky potato bugs or the weeds among the foliage—"a handy chore for those of us little ones built close to the ground," grownups grinned.

The patch prepared, we cut up the seed potatoes making sure each piece had an eye. With our pails full of eyes, we focused on the twine strung to keep the garden and us in line. One of us walked backward along that line digging holes with a spade, while the other dropped a potato eye in the hole, dragged her foot to cover it with dirt, stepped on it, and moved to the next hole back and forth, back and forth until we ran out of potato eyes.

Grownups wisely took over the tricky task of hilling with a hoe when the plants began to flower because most of us "managed" clumsy chopping with the hoe pretending to hill. Too bad we didn't manage to weasel out of weeding or picking potato bugs. At least two well-spaced sessions of planting were staged each spring to stagger the harvest, which struck me as a threat to overdose us on vitamin D and peeling noses.

To shade our faces, we wore bonnets that stuck out stiffly (too much starch I thought). A limper piece of fabric hung down the nape of our necks and the entire creation tied under our chins protecting our fair complexions and our blonde heads from ultra-violet rays. Those bonnets didn't protect me from a mask of dreaded freckles, though. Worse, I fell for the outlandish notion foisted on me by cousin Emma and my four older sisters that freckles disappear after you rub your face with used, wet diapers. I went to the clothes hamper to give it a whirl. The freckles stayed. Besides, those blamed old bonnets were hot.

Sweet Corn, Snakes and Chairs

As grownups, we now think it was a ploy postured as a friendly competition when we were assigned the chore of hoeing and pulling up thistles and mustard between the stalks in rows of field corn. After the horse-drawn cultivator had been through the cornfields, we lined up at the headland, each working to rid his or her own row of the noxious offenders making sure to leave corn stalks intact. Neatness counted. Speed was encouraged.

By fall, stuffing ears of corn into the sheller and cranking like sixty produced a feeling of power. Forget that the faster we cranked the bigger the mess to clean up. With luck the chickens scurried to help with clean up. Shorn corncobs shooting out of the spout seemed magical. We could have used some of that magic when using knives to cut sweet corn off the cob with a knife during canning season.

One year the men also seeded a row or two of sweet corn in the field of feed corn for the livestock. At the right season, Ma had put the kettle on to boil water before she and I went to pick sweet corn for supper. Suddenly, she clutched my arm and pulled me aside with a loud whisper. "Rattle snake" rattling the rattler as much as me. Mr. Rattler and I skeddadled, leaving her alone to bring in the corn.

I was still feeling the shock from a few days earlier in a foot race around the house of squishing a snake under my bare foot. Ugh.

On summer evenings the suggestion of serving supper under the three maples on the side lawn suddenly stopped our slouching as though about to die from heat exhaustion. Instead of whining, "It's too hot and sticky to move," we leaped to set up a table and carry dining room chairs onto the lawn. Less enthusiastic were we, though, when she had us move those same chairs onto the lawn for a soap and water scrubbing preparing for a new coat of varnish.

Inside the house in the dining room, sitting on a Sears, Wards or Spiegel catalog atop a regular chair during meals meant one was *almost* grown up. Each of us started life at the dining room table wearing a bib and strapped into the highchair on the corner next to Ma where we learned to handle a spoon, fold our hands and babble along with the table prayer.

From there, one moved to the high stool on Pa's right where we learned how to cut our own meat and were expected to enunciate aloud the prayer. He predicted I would grow up to be an architect because of my obsession with measuring pieces of cheese to fit perfectly to the edge of the slice of bread. I felt special sitting next to him, but was eager to grow up enough for a regular chair. Then I could move beside Grandpa G. at the end of the table to be fascinated with his adeptness at pounding marrow out of a bone against his dinner knife.

Altar of the Lilac

At any hint of our plans for mock weddings and funerals during summers, the stately lilac arch in our front yard took on a solemn air. Planning weddings sent us to the attic in a dither to dig up discarded lace curtains, gowns of flimsy fabric, and at least one cast-off man's suit. Our brother, Paul, never did grow into those suits; and, rather quickly, he outgrew his willingness to play along at these girl games of Altar of the Lilac. He escaped to the barnyard for male company. Faced with this scarcity of Adam's apples, one of his sisters grudgingly took a turn at playing the groom.

Second oldest Velma knelt on the bottom front porch step fingering the top step as her pretend pump organ keyboard. We relished her histrionics of collapsing---copied from the pastor's daughter who really had fainted one Sunday during church, slumping on the pump organ during a hymn. We reveled in that memory with each of Velma's embroidered replays. "Here Comes the Bride" got full voice from our congregation, blithely insensible of an occasional passing car or hay wagon rumbling along the gravel road just yards away.

Contrived funerals also dug up thespian tendencies that may have better been buried. Oldest sister, our very own version of "Sarah Heartburn" Helen, draped in black, was magnificent as chief mourner. Since the little girls didn't always measure up to our standards of proper church behavior, one of them got to play dead under the lilac arch while the rest of us mourned through as many verses as we could remember of "Asleep in Jesus", "Abide with Me", or whatever came to mind. Once, after we recited "The Lord's my Shepherd" pig-tailed Lois segued into "Mary Had a Little Lamb." We big girls smirked at her. Lois flounced into the house for comfort,

Most afternoons, Ma announced naptime for herself and for us---over our objections that we weren't sleepy. She waved us away with, "You don't have to sleep, just lie down---and have a quiet time."

Banquets and Music Lessons

Melodramatic fainting and singing went along with the territory when we left the farm to move to St. Paul in 1942.

At the drop of a hint, Donna can still put on her "Eek! My pills!" fainting routine that brought wild applause in a one-act play we sisters put on as part of youth programs at church and at the annual Mother-Daughter Banquets. Each year our mother took bows as the mother with the most daughters; though not too proudly when during one play Donna entered the stage toting a bag of groceries that burst through the bottom of the bag and rolled every which way on stage. She gathered her wits, gathered the groceries, and true to the-play-must-go-on tradition her frantic unladylike bending all but mooned the audience.

At the farm, years earlier in Chatfield, the pharmacist's wife had asked to borrow our second-youngest sister, Marilyn, for the Mother/Daughter banquet at her ladies club. Marilyn was thrilled. Second-oldest sister Velma offered to take Marilyn along on a shopping trip to Rochester to buy a dress for the occasion. Marilyn forgot the shopping date with Velma. Baby sister, Meredith, got to go on the shopping trip, the new dress and got to go to the banquet..

In grade school group piano lessons had been offered, so 3rd grader Marilyn showed up and enjoyed three lessons until the bureaucrats caught on that she was not a paying member of the class. Not to worry, as a 5th grader she passed the music test and was assigned to play the clarinet because "we already had one in the house from Lilas's days in the band when she was in 5th grade." Marilyn took the clarinet along with the obligatory spit rag familiar to all clarinet players. She liked playing the clarinet, but liked recess more. Band Director, Mr. Arsers, often sent another band member to the playground to bring Marilyn in for practice. She conveniently *forgot* her clarinet lessons.

Helen and Velma were taken into town once a week for piano lessons. Pa splurged by making a deal for one of those new fangled *player* pianos. It was lovely in our living room. Putting the rolls in place, pumping a mile a minute and watching the keys dance out the tune drove us into a frenzy of music. Helen and Velma were allowed to use the player rolls only *after* they had practiced their lessons. A chart of the keys was slipped above the keyboard to teach the rest of us the names of the notes.

That piano got professional treatment by Don Meese, who came to redecorate our living and dining rooms, taking his breaks at the piano, to spill glorious music throughout the house. He enchanted us with music and humor, along with his creations on our walls using the stippling technique in shades of green and vermilion paint, which brought homemakers from miles around to see what Frieda Gehrke had done to her home. Don inspired us to buy sheet music. We'd ask the pianist in the music store to play our choices before purchasing — our own mini concert. Before buying a record, we took our choice into a sound-proof booth to try it on a Victrola.

On Mother's Day, 1938. In age order.

Boy Cousins and Scars

Paul basked in his unusual power of majority when Minnesota boy cousins visited—another signal for more buggy riding in the slough and around the windmill in our own yard. Things got more frolicsome at the sound of Uncle Otto's musical horn on his car with fancy sunshades announcing the arrival of four more boy cousins from Texas. Paul got roommates! These overnight guests tried to teach us to ride sheep and generally livened up daily chores. Years later these cousins showed Donna and me a grand vacation in Texas, including a turkey shoot in Mesquite country. Mil and I bagged a tom turkey---well, Mil shot it. I helped carry it back to camp.

Boy cousins helped us swing into action on the huge oak tree limb stretching over the county roadside ditch —perfect place to hang our rope swing with a short plank for a seat. We took turns to see who could push the hardest. A strong pusher could sail the swinger into ethercapacious with such a thrill it seemed a pity to come back to earth. One day as we swung, cousin Emma drove along the highway with Tante Vina. We waved. Emma waved, looked away from where she was going and steered their Studebaker into the ditch. Grateful for the excitement, we clustered around the car, relieved there were no injuries and basked in this welcome disruption in our day. How Emma explained to Uncle Tader how she happened to drive into a patch of weeds leaving a few scars on his prize car was never talked about.

We and the neighbor children used the open grassy slough across the county highway to pull and push the single-tree buggy taking turns giving each other rides. One of our rides got such a head of speed that no one noticed pixie Bee had fallen under a front wheel which ran over her stomach. We ran on. Spunky Bee assessed her injuries, decided she wasn't at death's door, picked herself up to catch up with us and complained about our callous neglect of her poor stomach for days, yeah, for years

"Race ya" was an almost daily dare, prompting foot races on the way home from school. Infant sister Marilyn's inner alarm clock went off at 4 every afternoon to be turned off by the first child home to pick her up to rock and sing to her. More days than not, I was that first child. Rocking Marilyn got me out of chores, especially helping with supper---must be her fault that I never took a shine to cooking.

Marilyn could also be blamed for my scraped knees. To be first to pick her up, I had committed the sin of running past neighbor boy Marvy. Enraged, he ran close enough to me to sling his jacket at my feet, tripping me. Down I went, skinning my knees. This flared the tempers of my older sisters, Helen, Velma and Bee. Next day at school they defended their little sister by broadcasting their own versions with, "You shoulda seen that big bully Marvy throw his jacket in front of her on purpose."

I proudly displayed my knee bandage of honor.

Gophers, Sexing Chickens and Haying

Minnesota Gophers' sports teams of today came by their name honestly and our brother Paul knew why. By the time he was in third grade he earned money for the family larder. Donna and I in fifth grade tagged along to the east pasture to trap gophers. Paul was the real trapper. Donna and I mostly dawdled rather than actually setting traps.

When we found a freshly dug mound, we fell to our knees and arranged the dirt by hand to place and hide the trap, careful not to snap off our fingers. Next day we checked the traps. On lucky days, Donna and I looked away while our kid brother removed the victim, an icky, often bloody, bunch of brown fur. Paul kept an eye out for empty Prince Albert tobacco cans to store the front legs of his quarry and present his booty to neighbor Roy Greenlee of the Jordan Township Board where he collected the bounty---5 cents per pair of front legs, a princely sum for a lad in the 1930's.

Paul was also useful for our hired man, Fred---sometimes referred to as the "hammered-down Dutchman" at Farm Bureau meetings. To solve his vertically challenged problem of hoisting cumbersome collars of harness onto the back of a one-ton draft horse, Fred threw the harness over his shoulder and climbed the ladder up the chute to the hay mow. Paul would lead a 17-hands-high bay, either Rex or Hector, under the haymow chute so Fred could drop the harness on the horse's back. The bay was now ready for us to wonder at the sight of him straining to haul heavy loads of boulders on the stone boat, similar to the stone boats used for training the famous Busch Clydesdales on the Grant Ranch in Missouri.

Sexing chickens had been profitable for Paul and effective in keeping him out of the pool hall while he waited to come of age to sign on as a Merchant Marine. Chicken sexing is the art of sorting through tiny puffs of yellow to cull future roosters from their egg-laying counterparts, which Paul did in the local hatchery. To learn this tricky maneuver, he rode a Greyhound bus to Shawnee, Oklahoma and spent several weeks in special studies for his certification.

Not until he was 35 years old did he confess to Ma that he had dared to hitchhike (forbidden in days of the Lindbergh kidnapping) from Shawnee to Omaha's bus depot. The citified lady behind the Omaha depot desk sized up this farm-grown lad coming up on his 15th birthday. She mothered him with, "I'll watch your things, you sleep on that bench in the corner, and I'll wake you in time for your bus in the morning." He did and she did.

Haying season had me watch for the chance to avoid housework and get my turn to drive either Twinkle or Tuff, our dapple grays. Either horse was hitched to a rope and pulley to lift forks loaded with hay from the hayrack up to the little door at the peak of the barn roof. With reins in hand, I walked beside the rope pulling that fork load of hay until the sound of the fork tripped with a click at that tiny door atop the barn.

Wrestling that long, dangling rope and not letting it tangle or slap my legs kept me hopping as I drove the horse back to the barn waiting for the man on the hayrack to plunge the fork into the hay and call "Giddyap." The horse picked up on that cue and tugged along until we got to the end of our rope. Hearing the click, the horse stopped, we turned ready for the next trip, the next and the last until all of the hayracks were empty and the haymow was full. That haymow turned into a gigantic playpen on stormy days. It's a wonder we weren't plagued with hay fever from the clouds of dust we stirred sliding down haystacks.

Even more tempting for romping was a granary full of new grain, but that was strictly forbidden territory since the grain, like quicksand, could swallow one to an early grave. A half-empty silo beckoned, despite having to gasp for air as we climbed the ladder inside that hot, airless vertical dungeon in the sky. Grappling for a foothold on those shallow steps and inhaling acrid fumes heightened our adventure. Then there was the day I got caught trying to climb (also forbidden) the windmill ladder with Mother warning, "if you break a leg don't come running to me." Oh, how that platform at the top beckoned.

Another forbidden temptation was smoking---we were too young, anyway. We tested our manual dexterity by helping the men "roll their own." Only rich men smoked ready-mades, we decided. More intriguing was a brief phase that smokers went through of smoking cigarettes through a contraption with a tube, a bubble and water. How that worked puzzled us, but it did keep Paul supplied with empty Prince Albert tobacco cans.

Frieda's ER

Plenty of excitement came the day Twinkle and Tuff, hitched to the drag, spooked and turned into runaways. A drag tooth bit into Twinkle's rear left leg. No one remembers what spooked them. Twinkle's medical emergency, outside of the realm of Frieda's ER in her kitchen, intrigued and huddled us each evening when Twinkle was tied to the windmill post where they dressed her ugly wound. Donna's nursing tendencies let her watch. I peeked between my fingers.

The Emergency Room, open 24/7, housed strips of old sheets to bind up injuries amid tears of pain—real or pity pandering. Colliding with barbed wire caused injuries each spring while hanging May baskets or in winter while sledding. Velma's 90-year old face still shows scars from the day she and Bee flopped on their stomachs onto the sled, but couldn't get momentum. Helen gave them a running push, lost her footing, landed on top, sinking all three below the crust of snow with Velma's cheek scraping icy snow into the barbed wire fence.

Like freeway commuters, we pushed closer to gawk at injured siblings, partially covering our eyes uttering, "ooh yuckie." With hot soapy water Ma washed away enough blood to see the severity of the wounds, carefully laid in place the layers of lacerated flesh, bound up the whole thing with strict instructions, "keep it clean and don't tear the bandage until I change it tomorrow."

The top shelf of a kitchen cupboard turned into a medicine cabinet with Iodine, Carbolic Salve, liniment, Cod Liver oil, cough syrup, and Absorbine, Jr. Most of these were delivered by the Watkins Man's traveling pharmacy, also offering spices, flat irons, and assorted household items. Pink eye, stings from bees or burn nettles and removing wood ticks waited their turn with tweezers, vinegar, baking soda, etc. Twice, Yellow Jaundice laid me out in the downstairs bedroom. The special attention made it almost worth those feverish sessions.

"Feed a cold and starve a fever" was bandied about with confident abandon making it seem like a medical miracle---right up there with putting hot goose fat in our ears. She also tied heated diapers around our heads for our earaches. Hideous! Worse, we had to miss school.

Quarantines for scarlet fever, measles, chicken pox and whooping cough were tended to by our parents with neighbors stopping by on their way to town for a what-to-buy list left in our mailbox. Later their deliveries piled up outside the back porch door.

When not practicing medicine in her own kitchen, Ma played the role of maternity patient. For these blessed events we children were mysteriously shuttled off to Tante Vina's to spend the night. Next morning we were surprised to find a new baby in the family.

Baby number eight, seventh daughter, Lois, slipped into our lives through the hired man's bedroom floor heating register in the kitchen ceiling above the cook stove. We woke to an unusual commotion downstairs, shuffled out of bed in our flannel nighties aiming our eyes and ears at that register to make out sounds. An ailing kitten or puppy in the warming oven? No, sounded like a baby crying. Patient and Doc Clifton had pulled off this blessed event while we slept upstairs.

Only one of us landed in a hospital. Bee's tonsils and adenoids acted up. She landed across the state line in La Crosse, Wisconsin. We coveted her diet of ice cream and special attention. Our reward came when Aunt Dora's family of La Crosse invited us to spend the weekend. She seated us at the dinner table and said, "Oh, did I miscount? There's an empty chair. Who's missing?" They found me in the garage asleep in the back seat of the Cadillac. Middle-child syndrome? At least, *someone* missed me. I always did like Aunt Dora.

Radio, Movies and Barn Fire

Not only had Uncle Tader and Tante Vina Meyer's home been our first stop for hanging May baskets in the 1920s and 30s, their home was the first place the magic of radio penetrated our lives. Their radio, powered by a generator in their basement, stretched our world into the adventures of Amos 'n Andy, Fibber McGee and Molly and Jack Benny. By turn, two or three of us pasted ears against the raspy speaker to catch every word.

By the time baby Meredith turned three, we had moved to town, where electricity and the luxury of our own radio rattled her if this gadget didn't hop to when she pleaded "Let's listen to Blondie."

The Meyer family thrilled us by inviting us to see silent films projected against their white house. We dragged chairs and stools from the house or lounged on blankets to wait for night to turn black enough to roll the film. No one minded the clapboard pattern of the house showing through every scene.

Then came the day we went with them to silent movies inside a real theatre where we also saw Hal Roach's "Little Rascals." Never could I have imagined that decades later I would have the fun of photographing Mr. Roach at his 90th and 100th birthday parties where Howard Keel led a roomful of movie celebrities singing "Happy Birthday" at each of these events.

Our first talkie, "The Trail of the Lonesome Pine," starred Sylvia Sydney, Henry Fonda and Fred MacMurray. Fifty years later I still had a crush on Mr. MacMurray when I photographed him for Bel-Air Country club's newsletter. We chatted about his ranch up north in California's famous redwood trees---not far from where I live now. He asked me to pray with him when he was diagnosed with throat cancer.

At these movies, second oldest sister, Velma, was so smitten with handsome Randolph Scott, she fell into a phase of clipping pictures of movies stars from magazines, to the delight of her sisters and girlfriends. `

Meyers two boys, Elmer and Melvin, and three girls, Verna, Edna and Emma, were just enough older than we to shore up our imaginations making us feel like those swells who wear spats, that we read about.

Verna's tales of her trip to Chicago for the 1934 World's Fair had our mouths agape. The pictures she came back with shivered me thinking about really and truly seeing that big city.

On some summer afternoons these girl cousins invited us for lemonade. We spiffed up in afternoon dresses (to my sisters' relief, I shed my bib overalls with ragged knees). We walked the mile to sit under our cousins' wide snowball tree to gossip and giggle over sweets and pink lemonade. The highlight of these afternoons was using their indoor plumbing. The indoor toilet was reserved for number one only---for number two we used the back house. Something to do with clogging the plumbing, I supposed.

Almost as much fun with them was setting up quilt frames braced on tops of dining room chairs. This made a tent to sit under as soon as our mothers had stretched out the backing material for a new quilt and had put down the batting and padding. We smaller girls got the job of poking the needles back up to those handier than we were with needles and yarn. Above us, they tied and knotted the yarn to secure the patchwork designs the grownups had arranged from sewing scraps. Tons of quilts over the years made for frolicsome bedtime games as we identified each square, strip or diamond-shaped fabric to guess in which dress or suit it had been in its former life.

One haunting night the call "BARN FIRE at Sabatkes!" sent our entire family down to Meyers. We watched the blaze a half-mile down the ravine from their house. Big kids hunched over the little ones at their upstairs bedroom windows. Our own fear and hysteria matched that of the livestock scattering.

"Look at the horses panic," one of us screamed.

"The chickens are skittering across the lawn."

"They don't know whether to run or fly," we snickered uneasily.

"Their wings might fan the flames."

"Don'   t be silly, they're too far away from the fire."

Edna and Verna calmed us with whispers of bravado. Elmer and Melvin had joined our fathers and neighbors. Those firefighters made eerie silhouettes against the bleary horizon as they moved in syncopation herding horses and cows to safety; all the while hauling and spouting water to smother the shooting flames of orange, red, yellow and blue.

By sunrise they had saved the neighbor's house and other farm buildings. That barn's empty stone foundation stood like a spooky, lonely tomb for years after the smoke faded.

Milking and Play Acting

Raising "pretty little milk maids in a row" wasn't Pa's style. "Milking gives girls big knuckles," he declared.

He also frowned on us straining to reach top shelves lest we damage our inner female paraphernalia. Our three oldest sisters were taught to milk, but allowed to milk only now and then, never taking a daily turn. Fourth and fifth daughters, Donna and my fingers were too small to squeeze hard enough to produce milk, so we got the safer job at the other end of the cows. I'd drop an armful of hay at the head of each cow with Donna right behind carrying a pan to scoop a supplement we called "frosting". We topped off that fun by pulling ourselves up to hang over the stanchions to watch the milking. When brother Paul's fingers grew big enough, his masculine knuckles were put at risk by milking every morning and night in Minnesota's humid summer or icy winter.

Washing those milk pails and cream cans in scalding, soapy water past our elbows was no picnic. Ma supervised, or took over, that job as sanitation was paramount. The other tricky job she handled herself was washing the dining room lantern-style gas lamp's chimney with its fragile wick. But we got to wash the kerosene lamps' glass chimneys every Saturday, or mid week if someone dared smoke up the chimneys by turning up the wick too high.

Washing windows didn't thrill us, especially the January day Pa met the train to pick up the new hired man. We washed the bottom half of the cloak room window to size up this stranger when they would drive in the yard.

Ma rebuked, "Don't be silly, girls, he may be too tall for your window's clean bottom half. Get back to churning butter and cleaning the bedrooms---with more than a lick 'n a promise."

We flitted from the dining and living room windows for signs of our horse and cutter coming down the Baier hill. When the men finally did drive across the frozen lawn yard, the hired man stood up in the cutter, his face vanishing behind the unwashed upper half of the window. Guess who laughed and flashed a serves-you-right look at us silly girls.

Helen went back to churning butter. This was a one-girl job. We took turns at that tedious shaking of fresh milk in a Mason jar wishing for solid pieces to appear, promising a chunk of butter. A few years later, the Creamery's truck from town picked up our cream, churned it into butter and returned it in two- or three-gallon crocks, which we stored on planks in the well-house tank (our version of an icebox) fed by windmill water so icy it made our teeth ache. No iceman delivered ice to farms. Each winter as soon as Bear Creek on our 50-acre woods froze hard enough, the men chipped, chopped and sawed chunks of ice hauling them to the icehouse nestled under a thick stand of trees where the ice was smothered in sawdust.

The icehouse was directly across the county highway from the Township Hall where May Day play-day, community meetings, concerts and play productions were staged. A day or two before May Day the man from the township who mowed highway ditches, came in with his team and mower to spiff up the lawn around the town hall for the Maypole celebration, picnic and competitions with children from the small neighboring one-room schools. Teachers mixed it up with the children in egg races, three-legged and wheelbarrow races, running, broad jumping---often winding up the day with a game of softball work-up followed by awarding ribbons to the day's winners.

That Township Hall still stands. This stone building with more than foot-wide walls, had window sills deep enough for babies and toddlers to curl up for naps while parents socialized or conducted meetings. One fall we giggled and boasted that our very own father was to play the lead in a play of a community production staged in that Hall.

I don't remember the name of the play or what role he played, but I do remember I didn't know if I felt proud because he was such a big hit with the crowd or more pleased that his many bows kept me up past my bedtime.

Fletcher Gray and Ice Cream

At milking time, the minute Paul, age 5, and I, age 7, leaned against the barn door latch we heard the herd of 21 dairy cows mill about in the barnyard eager to squeeze through the door. Long-standing manners took over as these bovine ladies stood aside to let their sister, Fletcher Gray, be first in line. Fletcher seemed to smile as she sashayed to her stall at the top of the row of stanchions. Then the others hustled to poke their heads into their stalls to chew their supper of hay.

The men clapped shut each stanchion before they picked up pails to begin milking. Fred, the hired man, got to milk everyone's favorite, Fletcher Gray—only cow with a name. No one remembers why or where that came from. Fred carried a three-legged stool to Fletcher's rear right side and sat down clamping a pail with a bail between his knees.

He squeezed and pulled on Fletcher's teat of her mammary gland, usually called her bag. Paul and I hung around for the fun of having Fred tip a stream of milk into our wide-open mouths. After Fletcher's bag was empty he poured the milk into a large can already filling with milk from the rest of the herd. Ice cream doesn't come from whole milk, so the men lugged the large can to our de Laval cream separator in the well house. They hoisted the milk into a silver bowl perched atop the separator. Two spouts came out of the bowl. Inside the bowl was a stack of metal plates.

We took turns cranking the separator as fast as our arms would go, spinning the plates in the bowl throwing the cream apart from the milk by centrifugal force. We loved saying "centrifugal" almost as much as we loved the cranking. This shot the cream into a spout flowing into a skinny can, about as tall as a preschooler. The skim milk drained through the other spout into a can about the size of a squat first- or second-grader.

Now we had our cream, but still no ice cream. Time to go the half-mile up the road to the icehouse for that ice the men had chopped from Bear Creek in our woodland during winter. Next, it was time to mix the ice cream recipe while we waited for the fun of cranking again---this time the handle on the ice cream freezer.

Lucky for sisters Lois, Marilyn, Lilas, Donna and me there was ice available for cranking up a batch of ice cream for our winter birthdays. But, when Meredith and Paul's birthdays in May, Helen's in July, Velma and Bee's in September came around only rattlesnakes would be found in the secluded icehouse.

Ice cream socials are still my favorite social events. Donna and I jumped at the chance to paint the backhouse for Aunt Rosie who was hosting a big ice cream social. She was my adorable Godmother, who also made the best devil's food cake in the world. We worked hard not to splatter paint on the grass and trees knowing that in a few days their front lawn would turn festive with bouquets of flowers and colorful tables and chairs for one of their many ice cream socials. Donna took bows on our artistry on the back house while I lapped up ice cream.

The Pail

"Who got hurt?" I blurted when I spotted the pail of bloody rags soaking in water by the cistern on a summer morning in 1929.

No one answered. I ran around the corner of the house yelling, "Is it butchering day?"

Still no answer. I looked in the barnyard for Freddie, the butcher, whose beard always reminded me of last year's bird nest. Silly me, of course Freddie wasn't around. If it had been butchering day I would have heard and seen the squealing hogs staggering in the path around the windmill until they collapsed from having had their throats slit–"for clean bleeding" the grownups explained each year.

How dumb of me to not notice the men weren't hauling boilers of hot water to the machine shed where on butchering days they hung sides of beef or hogs. I ran on. Surely someone beside me saw those bloody rags in that pail beside the cistern pump.

I asked again, "Who got hurt?" No answer. Finally, older sisters Velma and Bee smirked and muttered what sounded a bit like cursing. Except, we were not allowed to curse. The big girls turned away from this inquisitive second grader ranting with questions. Their rebuff sent me slouching off the lawn to pout where, at the gate, I broke off an evergreen twig to amuse myself making swirls in the livestock watering tank.

After the men had come in for dinner and gone back into the fields for the afternoon's work, I noticed the pail was gone. I noticed Velma hanging out scraps of sheets and old pillowcases on the clothesline in the bright afternoon sun. Still, I didn't put two and two together about those rags in the pail and her white laundry.

My curiosity did peak years later in Sunday School when we learned about the woman of great faith who touched the hem of Jesus' garment to heal her disease of twelve years of an issue of blood.

Then came the day when that Sunday School curiosity matured to full flower. I got the answer about the pail. Thank God, by then sanitary napkins were readily available and I could even say 'period' , ' the curse', 'pregnant', and 'menopause' with men in the room.

Tankee and Happy Jack

"Time to go to the fields," came from the kitchen when Ma stood in the doorway with a packed lunch during harvest season each mid-morning and again in afternoon.

"I get to pump today," was heard as one of us children ran to the windmill while others gathered clean Mason jars or buckets. Our water brigade in bare feet toe danced (too stubborn to put on shoes) trying not to draw blood as we sidestepped stubbles in the grain field left by the blades of the big red Harvester grain binder. One could get dizzy watching that binder's tall wheel of slats bend the grain to slice it off to be tied into bundles with twine and spit out the bundles ready for the shocking crew.

Shocking grain was adult work: prop bundles heads up against each other in teepee fashion, break one bundle to form a cap to protect the grain against moisture. We looked forward to the time to shock flax on the back forty, usually a couple of weeks after barley, wheat and oats had been harvested. Shocking flax needed no capping, so we were allowed to help. Flax heads of little balls (raw material for linen) works well when boiling the seeds to make hair-setting lotion. These balls protect themselves from moisture. After the shocking and harvesting, our excitement built waiting for the bonfire in the field to burn the long, stringy flax straw.

Flax straw makes lousy bedding for the livestock. Imagine trying to snuggle into bed sheets of raw linen and you get the itchy picture.

Threshing season commotion made us giddy. We couldn't wait for our turns to ride with Tankee, our sporty cousin Melvin, the water carrier for the steam engine from Bear Creek a mile away. He hauled an elephant-size oblong water tank mounted on a wagon pulled by his sorrel team. If your day to ride with Tankee (sometimes getting to hold the reins) happened also to be your day to blow the dinner or supper whistle on the steam engine you were really living it up. Uncle Tader or Pa, which ever was boiler tender, would boost us to the platform of the steam engine to pull the whistle cord. They shared ownership of the steam engine, water tank and threshing machine. As the grain ripened they'd call a Town Hall meeting to agree on dates for their machinery to move from one farm to the next, harvesting all fields in the neighborhood.

Pa below. Above, Grandpa Gehrke, Fred
holding me, Velma, Helen, Bee and Donna

Happy Jack, a lanky, good-natured hobo, spiced our lives with his romantic travel tales when for successive summers he showed up at harvest time. We tried to mimic his long-legged lopes and jumps that we imagined had landed him aboard cross-country freight trains. Our attempts gave us the giggles.

Decades later, Glen, our former hired man and jolly neighbor, said, "I remember all the men looked forward to threshing days at Frieda's house, because your mother was the best cook in the neighborhood."

We agreed that slaving over a dishpan of potatoes to be peeled, shelling peas into the aprons across our laps, stringing and slicing beans, and sloshing up to our elbows in soapy dishwater had been worth it after all. But, my oh my, how we moaned and groaned at the time, constantly keeping eyes 'n ears alert not to miss our turns with Tankee, blow that dinner whistle, or miss the chance for a trumped up frivolity.

Setting the dining room table, stretched to the limit with extra leaves, for two sittings at dinner and again at supper gave us a chance to show a bit of grace rather than hustling to clear the table for the next batch of threshers. Waiting on table got us better acquainted with some men we seldom saw, while listening to man talk---which they kept in check out of respect for Frieda and her girls. After dinner the men stretched out under the shade of our maples for a breather, some snored, before returning to the fields. After supper they went directly home, leaving us with the stacks of dirty dishes.

With the clean kitchen closed, we'd step out to take deep drags of night air and count low hanging stars while dreaming of next year's harvest.

Cultivating Cooperation

Pa clapped a straw hat on my 9-year-old head and thrilled my socks off (well, I was already barefoot). He lifted me and plunked me on the back of Hector, the one-ton bay, harnessed to the walking plow. Riding/steering Hector excused me from garden work that day, the next, and every day until we finished that field. Better yet, no housework for me, especially dreaded cooking.

Cooking still doesn't thrill me. Recently, a sister presented me with a, "If it fits in the toaster I can cook it " plaque.

When the walking plow broke down, he asked, "Want to walk in with me for parts, or wait in the shade by the windbreak?" He reached to lift me down, but I waved him off and laid back on Hector's broad back "about an axe handle and a half across" an expression we'd heard from men describing someone else's wife. I slid the straw hat over my face and napped. So did Hector. He lulled me swishing flies with his tail. An occasional ripple of his hide, when a fly bit him, tickled my legs.

When the sweet-corn patch needed cultivating, Donna and Paul and I took turns. One rode 3/4-ton mare Twinkle, one guiding the walking plow; and the third snoozed under oak and walnut trees across the fence.

As a lad in the lower elementary grades, a bit taller than a yardstick Paul made an impressive, though peculiar picture handling 4,000 lbs. of horses, the bay team, Hector and Rex, hitched to the seeder, the drag or the harrow. The 3/4-ton each dapple grays, Twinkle and Tuff, were child's play for Paul. When the green John Deere tractor materialized on our farm, that, too dwarfed, but didn't deter, him. He was one gutsy guy.

In grade school, Paul, two years my junior, played his masculine card when he announced to me, "I am the boss of you". His reasoning: "You're the *youngest* of the five oldest, but I'm the *oldest* of the five youngest." Go figure. Either way, he and I were proverbial middle children; both neglecting to feel neglected.

One day Pa gave into my pesky begging and put the reins of the dapple grays, Twinkle and Tuff, into my hands to drive the corn cultivator. This was one of the softer horse jobs, even though that seat was iron. What a thrill to feel all that power coming back to me through the reins. With my eyes glued far ahead to the rows of corn between the horses, I'd sneak glimpses between my feet, fascinated by the earth curling away from the plowshares. My concentration was so intense---to be deserving of his trust in me---I hadn't noticed he was in the adjacent field keeping an eye on me. Nor, did I, a slip of a girl, mind the heat from the hard metal seat air conditioned with holes.

Years later when learning to drive a car, it struck me that my corn cultivating instincts kicked in; outfitting me with space and movement sense from having eyeballed those precise 90-degree turns from the headlands into the next rows to avoid pulling up tender stalks of corn.

Another job called for driving Twinkle and Tuff on the hay mower. This could be handled by a willing youngster with enough good sense and strength to lower and lift the sickle. Keeping hands and feet away from the moving sickle blades kept one alert.

Mowing the lawn, a three-man job---often assigned to Donna, Paul and me---was a lesson in getting along with each other whether you like them or the job. Power mowers had not been born. Our push mower called for push and pull. The two pullers climbed inside a rope tied to the front cross bar between the mower wheels, making sure the rope was long enough to keep our feet well ahead of the mower blades. The pusher's job was to steer and keep the blades tilted down into the grass. Two pullers getting up a head of steam tended to yank the blades skyward.

Taking turns as pusher, or as left- or right-side puller, worked well only if we three were in a good mood and no one got huffy about how the other guy was doing his/her job. Tell-tale patterns in the lawn left by the mower and how well we had steered around bushes and flower beds determined if we passed inspection. To avoid redoing part or all of the job, especially in July or August in muggy Minnesota, cultivating the art of cooperation quickly took hold with us.

Good thing, too. Cooperation helped us keep the kitchen's wood box filled beside the cook stove. Paul, Donna and I pulled our little wagon to the woodpile beside the sheep shed to pick up wood that had been sawed and split. After picking up pieces that we judged to be the right size to fit in the front door of the stove we crisscrossed layers in the wagon.

Donna usually said, "Put up more side boards, so we can get by with one trip." We poked kindling pieces on end along the sides, added another layer, then two of us laid arms across the load saying to the puller, "Go slow, so it

doesn't slip on our feet."   Never lost a
toe or broke a foot.

Cow Pies, Cricket and Watermelon

Around 1744, three-legged milking stools were used for bases in baseball, according to William Safire in his Sunday New York Times Magazine column in 2005. In the 1920's and 30's, rather than milk stools, we used dried cow pies for bases while playing softball in Gehrke's pasture where Bear Creek ran through our family's woods. All school and church picnics were held in our pasture, ideal for brisk group games.

The ideal cow pie is crispy dry to keep the game clean for runners sliding into bases. Cow pies may have helped popularize what is hailed as our nation's favorite pastime played with bases, bats and balls. Those early balls may have been made from cowhide. Why not? Footballs are called pigskins. Who knows? Cows may be able to milk their fame for aiding and abetting America's autumn madness, our World Series.

At home, when not enough of us children were around for a game of softball, we laid out designs of houses with sticks and bricks under a long canopy of the concord grape arbor. This went well until a clumsy foot dragged across a wall or someone mistook a window for a door squelching our well laid plans. Anyway, by that time our lips and teeth may have turned purple from feasting from our "roof" of juicy concords.

From there we might play ante-I-over-the-backhouse (toilet, outhouse or privy) playing catch by throwing balls over the backhouse. I liked it better when we went to the orchard of Dutchies, Greenings and Wealthy apples to compete in slinging apples into the pigsty. We sharpened sturdy twigs to pierce windfalls and tried to outdo the other slingers.

Even more better (as I used to say), the pig barn of heavy stone gave us hiding places in the deep window sills and doorways where we ate forbidden green apples rubbed on the live stocks' saltlick. We resorted to that gross saltlick only if we couldn't tempt one of the little girls to sneak the saltshaker from the kitchen before causing suspicion about what we were up to. Big deal—we were found out when one or two of us got sick and threw up during the night.

To challenge ourselves for a new game, we came up with not-so-cricket cricket—apologies to the British. Our cricket course began with gouging a narrow, deep canoe-shaped hole in the lawn and placing a stout, short, stick across it. The idea was for each player at bat, holding a slimmer stick a yard-long or so, to flick that small stick lying across the hole as far and as high as possible with those in the field trying to catch it. Our brother Paul was the best stick flicker.

Earning points by catching the stick was serious business, but even more serious was fielders protecting their own eyes. No wonder we were quickly steered to safer chores that needed doing when we got caught digging a hole for cricket. Grownups heartily encouraged us back to safer softball---work-up we called it---with each player moving up a position after each out. Work-up was played on that same cricket course on the side lawn on summer evenings after the men came in from the fields and supper dishes had been washed. Pa pitched. Ma umpired. We took turns as catcher, first, second and third basemen, shortstops and outfielders.

Even worser (another of my limp expressions) the biggest threat to our safety was Donna at bat. She was a strong hitter, but she was a "hooker." It went something like this. When Donna stepped to the plate, and Paul, squatting in the catcher box, called out, "Let 'er rip!" it was the signal for Ma to leave the umpire box to take up a defensive position at the bathroom window.

The pitcher wound up and let go a slider. Donna swung and hit one of her best. She ran past Bee at first base, past Velma at shortstop, zipped by Helen at second, but missed Lilas at shortstop. She had gone to the bathroom to retrieve the ball in case Ma had fumbled. Donna took this chance to run past Lois on third and slide home SAFE while outfielders Marilyn, baby of the family Meredith, and I moved up a notch. Note the shattered bathroom window on the cover of this book.

After all outs the call came, "Time out for watermelon!" One or two melons waited for us in the cooler tank up at the well house. We circled in the yard to feast with juice trickling down our arms followed by a seed-spitting contest.

A calmer and safer after-supper event was Ma bringing out the Bible History book and sitting on the grass in front of the lilac arch at the top of the drainage ditch where we could hang our legs. We raced for the choice place next to her for the best view of the pictures of Daniel in the Lion's Den, Shadrack, Meshach and Abednego in the fiery furnace, or the Three Wise Men dressed to the nines. Aside from the fascinating stories, her fluency with names like Melchizedek, Nebuchadnezzer,

Epaphroditus and Mesopotamia made exotic sounds that drew our eyes to her clever lips. After quick trips to the backhouse, a stop at the sink, we shuffled up stairs to bed to absorb the silence of the night with crickets to sing us to sleep.

Our Woods and Picnics

It was fairytale time when we went to The Woods. Apart from shady oaks and maples there were walnut and butternut trees producing bountiful harvests each fall. Nutting was a big event; though, removing husks, cracking shells and digging out the stubborn nut meat left stubborn greenish brown stains on our fingers. The stains faded by the time nut-filled cookies and cakes came out of the oven or platters of divinity topped with a nut were passed around.

Billy Gamble, a mild-mannered bachelor with a spectacular beard and no teeth, lived at the edge of our Woods in a small house straight out of a story book which sent out marvelous aromas from his Mulligan stew. Billy's (he was the only adult we called by his first name) Mulligan stew was standard fare at neighborhood pinochle parties. He almost never joined in the pinochle. He was content to mind his pot of stew, now and again showing his toothless approval at the noisy card players' twaddle drifting into the kitchen.

A natural spring cascaded from a grassy hillside on the woodland. Kneeling to scoop up water so cold it hurt the teeth brought squeals of ecstasy. When we ran down the slippery slope to Bear Creek stepping around twigs and poison ivy, I grabbed a handful of my cheek in each hand as a safety throttle. Don't ask. But, it worked for me. We fished for crappies and proudly presented our catch to be pan fried for supper.

Wading and splashing in the creek got us through sticky July afternoons and the dog days of August. Not an Esther Williams among us. Decades later, my daughter, Jane, saw a classmate from her water ballet group in Santa Monica, California interviewed on television. "No wonder she's such a great swimmer! I had no idea she's Esther Williams' daughter."

Driving the car into the riffles of the creek made short work of washing cars. Two or three of us tall enough to reach the top and middle to do doors and the spare tire hooked on the back got the job done. Preschoolers joined in with a cleaning rag "because you're built for tires,"

Pa built a bench covered in plush that fit between the front and back seats (our version of jump seats) in the Cadillac so all 12 of us had a seat. The baby on a lap on the front seat, one of the big girls sat in the middle. Four sat across the back seat holding two little ones and two middle-sized people sat sideway on the bench.

A clearing in The Woods was perfect in size and shape for a kitten-ball diamond, as well as space for three-legged and egg races, etc. at annual school and church picnics. One church picnic exposed to the world my outlandish appetite for ice cream—aided and abetted by Pa who resolved to see if his daughter would ever get her fill of ice cream. He told the men working with him in the refreshment stand to keep track of how many ice cream cones I came for--he would settle up my bill at closing time. Seven times I came for a cone, puzzled and delighted at my good fortune. The eighth time, I was turned away–only because the ice cream was gone. A dream come true.

A couple of years before, I'd walked into the barn while Fred, the hired man, was milking our favorite cow Fletcher Gray. He directed streams of milk into my mouth. Giggling, I said. "Since Fletcher is a Brown Swiss, how about chocolate milk.?" *That* dream never came true.

Picnics included a softball or kitten ball game of work up. A bat and ball were part of the menu, right up there with potato salad, chicken, pickles, pies and cakes. Empty pie or cake pans, a stump of a tree limb or something out of somebody's car trunk marked the pitcher's mound, catcher's box, or home plate. Sometimes the three bases were courtesy of our herd of brood cows. Sliding into base could take on an element of surprise as not all cow pies are equal.

Then the day came that Bang's Disease spread throughout that herd of cows during their dry season. This, along with   the 30 hogs with cholera, marked the beginning of the end of farming for us.

Pie Tins and Mad Bull

As an infant, Lilas had napped in a dresser drawer to keep sawdust and nails from falling on her. In 1927 carpenters demolished most of our old 1 and ½ story house and built a four-story, five-bedroom home around, below, and above us as we carried on daily living. What fun when the contractor gave each of us children a turn to "help" by pounding a nail in the front porch floor.

Each morning the old wood kitchen floor was scrubbed with hot water before putting the baby down to play. To protect her from splinters, Lilas was put in a pie tin that let her scoot wherever she pleased. Three sisters later, this same pie-tin maneuver gave mobility to Meredith, the baby of the family. By then shiny hardwood floors of the newly built house allowed Meredith to whip around on what we had staked out as our race track from kitchen to dining room to living room to master bedroom and back to the kitchen. She's been speeding ever since

Lila's petite stature, curly hair and baby doll face had the carpenters, hired girl and hired man picking her up and fussing over her. As a first grader, she was carried to school on neighbor boy Marvy's back. As teenagers, brother Paul (two and half years older than Lilas) was assigned to see her home after school dances before he took his girl friend home. He was well paid for his trouble. Lilas spent hours and hours drop kicking a football for him out in the yard.

Paul was charged for keeping toddler Lilas inside the fenced lawn. One day she slipped through Paul's net and wandered into the barnyard where our gander flew on Lilas's shoulders and pecked the back of her head. Helen and Velma rescued Lilas, while the rest of us steered clear of that *spossy* gander with his long, skinny neck stretched out "all the better to hiss at you." But, if you want goslings to keep a steady supply of feathers and down for feather beds and fluffy pillows, or to enjoy next year's Christmas goose, you keep a gander.

Likewise, if you want milk and T-bone steaks, you keep a bull. A Brown Swiss bull held forth in the pasture just beyond the berry bushes behind the back house. Donna, Paul and I made sport of the bull by repeatedly pushing the flat of our hands against the fence until he snorted and pawed---then, we'd run away. One day we pushed our luck. He not only snorted and pawed, he butted against the fence and bellowed. Ma heard the dreaded bellowing, bolted out of the house and spoiled our sport by pointedly placing the flat of her hand on our backsides. The bull was rescued by moving him to a pasture beyond our influence.

FDR's WPA had not stopped a cluster of farm auctions seeming to happen in gloomy, wet weather. Three or four of us rode in the buggy to Oakeys' sale a mile away where we slid and slipped around rolled up linoleum floor coverings and furniture, working our way to the potluck buffet while trying to make sense of the auctioneer's patter.

Too young to know what hit me, I do remember the sadness spreading over me and our home the day neighbor Eddie Marshall sat on our kitchen chair, his legs spread apart with his folded hands hanging between his knees mumbling something about money and foreclosure. A foreclosure moved us from the home, where Lilas and Meredith had scooted around in a pie tin. From this big house we moved to the tin house.

Marilyn tells of how on moving day, as a four-year-old, she treated herself to a "ride" on the living room rocking chair while it waited on the front porch to be loaded. For her, and the chair's safety she had been forbidden to sit in that rocking chair because she tended to exceed the speed limit in the living room upsetting the rocker and bruising herself. Surely there was no speed limit on the porch. She rocked away. She and the rocking chair flipped over. Unhurt, she ran away pleased with herself.

Marilyn guides Meredith's walking

Tin House and More Bull

While still in the big house, Donna and I had moved to Grandpa and Grandma K's home in town so we could attend twice-a-week catechism classes after school. By coincidence, the same Friday that our family moved from the farm our neighbor Mr. Hess had come into town to pick up his daughter Betty. He offered Donna and me a ride and came to Grandma's home to load our things, including the cello I was told to practice on before Monday. We headed for "the home place" eight miles out of town.

Three and a half miles out I shouted. "Stop, we live here!" Mr. Hess braked and shot a suspicious glance at me.

"Look," I squealed, "That's Helen and Velma's bedstead leaning against that tin house." A bedstead painted bilious green trimmed in pink couldn't possibly have a twin. It had been a 4-H project for the two older girls and now had finally gained some respect by earning its keep as a signal that sure enough we did live here. We ran into the house.

Perplexed, Ma dropped her spoon in supper's pot of Hungarian goulash. "How in the world did you get here?" We all laughed, all talked at once, and hauled in the tell-tale green and pink bedstead, but not before unloading the cello and waving off the bewildered Mr. Hess and Betty. Amid the move from our birthplace, word had not reached us, nor had Ma expected us home that weekend, hence no phone call.

On the farm we had a telephone in a wooden box hanging on the wall with a handle to crank long or short rings if you were calling a neighbor. The beauty, or bane, of this system allowed rubbernecking on as many as a dozen families' conversations. Our parents were the only ones tall enough to use the telephone without standing on a chair. To call anyone not on our line, we cranked a long ring for Central, gave her the number and she connected us. Two women, who were sisters, aggravated neighbors by tying up the party line to read the latest segment of their favorite magazine serials.

Fall rains on the tin roof of our new home lulled us to sleep. Then winter took hold. Many mornings we woke to frost designs on our blankets from our breath. Laying out tomorrow's underwear next to the bed became a nightly defense tactic against frigid air. Next morning, arms snaked out from under the covers pulling our underwear into bed. We became undercover quick-change artists.

That 3-1/2 mile walk to school developed muscles and lungs for Paul, Donna and me. We had an oilcloth book bag, which Paul and I took turns carrying---he took the most turns, while Donna and I grunted and giggled, as I helped her short legs negotiate a snowdrift. He and I also took turns making a path when snowplows hadn't been through to pile their magnificent banks of snow that formed vast, silent corridors sheltering us from the wind. Much of that winter poor Pa was plagued with severe pleurisy as well as depression I would imagine.

Lilas and Lois walked nearly a mile to a one-room school down the Neimeyer hill past Uncle Albert and Aunt Rosie's house. Lucky preschoolers Marilyn and Meredith got to play school at home where they bundled up and waddled like penguins frolicking in snowdrifts.

Our new landlord and neighbor a mile up the road licked his chops at the prospect of at least a couple of us girls making good matches for his two sons. Numerous invitations came to join them for card playing or shooting caroms and for midnight suppers. Returning the invitations turned us into experts at caroms, but not into brides. The moonlight walks between our two houses on white, winter nights are a fond memory.

The slushy, muddy spring that followed had Paul, Donna and me zig-zagging for a secure spot to put the next step for the 3 ½ miles to and from school. In spring, the Niemeyer hill, forced many cars to growl and whip their tails. More than once we were pulled free by Uncle Albert's chestnut team of geldings. That team pulled more than just the car. It was too muddy to step out in our Sunday shoes and clothes to lighten the load, letting the team drag our loaded car.

At the tin house, once again that dreaded bellow of a bull was heard. It was the very hour that fourth and second graders, Lilas and Lois, were to walk from school. Ma gingerly followed the sound and the clouds of dust from a bull's pawing and furious pacing. She reached the top of the hill to see two fences between her and the bull, but no fence between the bull and the road that the girls would be walking. They appeared at the top of the next hill. She waved and shouted. "Climb the fence." Lilas picked up a stick (to fight a bull?) took Lois by the hand, kept an eye on the bull, planning to duck into a culvert in case he out-ran them to the fence.

An "angel" bull from an adjacent pasture responded to the bellowing, ran toward the mad bull and locked horns with him through the fence. Lilas and Lois climbed the fence and were hustled into the house.

In a few minutes, Bee showed up at the door unexpectedly. Dismayed, Ma blurted, "How did you get past the bull?" Bee said, "A salesman happened along, spotted the bulls, and turned around to rescue me."

Next day, our second cousin Ed shot his deranged bull.

Coming of Age

On our confirmation morning, May 9, 1937, Donna and I carried our white shoes the 3½ miles to Grandma's where our dresses were already waiting for us. Grandma and Ma had designed and sewn our white dotted Swiss dresses; Donna's with a row of buttons down the front from neck to hem, mine with tiny grosgrain bows which must have been a pain to tie and stitch in place. Sprigs of Lilies of the Valley, picked from Grandpa K's. flower beds, pinned to our shoulders topped our classy outfits.

A week before confirmation while trying to ride a bike, I skidded on loose gravel and skinned a knee, but kept the bloody, gravel-filled knee hidden from Grandma. When Ma came to town in a day or two, she spied---or smelled---the yellowish-green knee. She scrubbed it with a brush and hot soapy water to the tune of my not-so-muffled screams. On confirmation day my weight instinctively shifted to the good knee at the altar rail.

The first year we were both eligible to vote, election day fell in the year that Donna was 22; I, 21. At the polls, she pleaded, "All my life teachers and preachers have called your name on the role first because yours start with A, I want to be first in voting." Seemed fair. She stepped into a voting booth and I waited for the next available booth. I voted, came out and looked for Donna. Finally, she appeared in a huff.

"My machine didn't work. I have to go in another booth," she muttered. Foiled again.

She *was* first to become a bride. Pa admits tears popped to his eyes seeing the Katzenjammer Kids at the altar, Fritz the bride, Hans the bridesmaid.

Donna was first to give birth, too. Sadly, their twins, Ginger and Connie, lived less than a week. Blissfully, she and Jim Kuykendall became parents of Charles, Carol and Paul through adoption.

Donna' s gift of empathy gives her "a thing" about and with all kids, human and/or animal. As a toddler when the back screen door banged behind her, baby chicks, ducklings, goslings and kittens came at full tilt. They peeped, waddled and squealed at her heels, even milling around her feet in the outhouse waiting for her to shake the dew from her hollyhock.

When she grew up to become a career girl it was not uncommon for neighborhood children in St. Paul to come to our door and ask, "Can Donna come out to play?" She went out to play.

Girls for Hire

Eldest sister, Helen, was the first of us nine girls to reach the hiring-out stage in the mid 1930's. Our neighbors, the Obers, had to be away. They hired Helen to harvest their vegetables, keep house and cook for the hired man on their farm. She asked me to keep her company. We picked and canned tomatoes for the entire two weeks.

She had graduated from junior high at St. John's Lutheran Parochial School in Wykoff, Minnesota and was making plans for high school. There was no school bus service for the eight miles from our farm to Chatfield High School. Superintendent George Potter canvassed the county armed with his cut-n-dried plan to recruit and defray costs for future high schoolers.

The upshot was that when classes began in fall Helen earned her board and room at the home of the barber and his family. Velma, earned her keep with the band director. Mr. Arsers' family. When he noticed Velma had a good ear for music, he taught her to play the base viol. She landed in the school band and in the town band to perform at Wednesday night summer concerts, where townspeople and farmers gathered in the park---some sitting in their cars, honking horns to applaud.

For these concerts, six-year-old sister Marilyn happily agreed to polish her white sandals. After all, this weekly event was to see and be seen, much the same as Saturday nights on Main Street when farm families came to town along with town folks for weekly shopping and to hang out in the barbershop, the pool hall, one of the two beer joints, the grain elevator, or to chat around lampposts. Our doctor's wife, Mrs. Clifton, and other town ladies drove down town early Saturday evening to claim prize parking places on Main Street. Mrs. C's spot was in front of McClintock's drug store. As the evening wore on, grownups and children car hopped to pick up more and fresher gossip.

When sister number three, Bee, reached high school age she worked and lived with Tuohys, a family of children outnumbering our own. The year Donna and I were in 8th grade was still our time to attend twice-a-week catechism classes in town.

Our parents rented a room, with no running water, for us five oldest girls at Mrs. Lynch's house. Her other three upstairs bedrooms were rented to high school students; two sisters and brother across the hall; two girls on one side of us; three high school boys on the other side of us. In our one room w/closet, we installed a double bed for Donna and me and a collapsible couch with two pull-up sides for Helen, Velma and Bee.

We girls threaded a path through the three boys' room down the back stairway to the outhouse, and carried water from the only upstairs faucet behind the boys' room. Each room had a hot plate for cooking and a washbasin for sponge baths. Gym days to take hot showers in locker rooms were heaven. No refrigeration, apart from Minnesota's windowsills. By the end of the week our tastiest menus were gone, often leaving us with homemade bread and stewed tomatoes or more bread and chocolate pudding (made from scratch—no mixes). The camaraderie in Mrs. Lynch's boarding house bred a model of respect and tolerance crowned with laughter and fond memories.

Pocket money, after expenses, from baby-sitting jobs was scarce, trying our ingenuity when invited to birthday parties. Since each often had our own set of friends, it worked fine to bring home our own gift (often a lace-trimmed hanky), leave it in the gift box and lend it to the next sister who needed a gift for her next invitation. I still have one hanky now looking like its own lace trim.

When the family moved into town our sophomore year, Donna did housework and baby sat after school and Saturdays at the dentist and the Grain Elevator owner's homes; I worked at the General Store manager's and Doctor Clifton's homes. We each were paid $1 a week. To pass the time—no TV those days--while baby-sitting, I was handed the mending basket to darn men's socks. In those days of scarcity, I couldn't imagine how anyone could own 30 pair of socks. Later, at Cliftons the pay was $1.25 a week, a free ticket to the Wednesday night movie, no babysitting, and no socks to darn.

My senior year, it was still $1.25 when I hired to clerk at the General Store on Saturdays from 8 in the morning to closing about 11 p.m. after farmers picked up their orders. Listening to Dorothy Collins, Giselle MacKenzie, and Sonny somebody, or was it Kenny Baker, on radio's The Hit Parade was a welcome perk. Lack of Self-serve markets with checkout scanners developed one's brains and brawn. Customers handed their list to me to gather items from the appropriate shelves, total the bill on an adding machine and make change in my head. Helping customers on the dry goods side of the store to select and try on clothes let me play fashion consultant for men and women.

In 1938 Lilas, 11, and Lois, going on 9, struck it rich when Pa promised if he won his bet on the Louis-Schmeling fight they could have the money. There was a lot of talk around the house about Sea Biscuit that same year, but I don't remember hearing about bets on that race. He won the prizefight bet. Lilas and Lois took their $5 to buy enough burgundy fabric for each of them to have a princess-style dress and ribbons for their hair; then off to Falgreens shoe store where they had money left for each to buy a pair of shoes.

Not always did Lois do well with money the night the carnival came to town. Lois lost her money throwing balls at moving ducks because she thought she *had* to do as the barker said. She came away with a see-no-evil, hear-no-evil, speak-no-evil statue of a monkey. Lilas soothed Lois by taking her on the merry-go-round until they missed their date with Ma and scared themselves silly walking home alone in the dark for one and half miles on a country road.

Thank God no one mistook them for "Girls for Hire."

Sour-Dough and Trains

As soon as the school term was over we moved from the tin house to a sheep ranch near Preston, the county seat, for a summer of adventure. On the sheep ranch we were enchanted with helping frail newborn lambs breathe under the direction of Dan, the one-armed sheepherder, who regaled us with outlandish tales about Mexico and let us take turns riding behind him on his horse.

Isolated from our school friends on the ranch, we were taught how to braid five strands for rag rugs by tying one end of rag strips to the spoke of a dining room chair back so we could each work independently to produce half dozen beautiful rugs that summer. Carding wool was also a new and absorbing fulfillment. I rather wished we had a spinning wheel to go a step further with the filmy, fluffy fabric created by clapping the wood paddles and pulling the wool to pad quilts. Walking to town on railroad tracks we learned to "keep our ears to

the ground" for oncoming trains. Their
routine sounds marked our days and
nights.

Stirred by the 6 o'clock Freighter
aromas of coffee and
sour-dough pancakes
wafting up the stairwell

We shoulder fishing poles
cross the sheep pasture
to Shoelace Creek
for the day's catch

No train in sight
dare we balance along
slick rails to cross bridge
before 9:30's Thruway?

Too late!
whistle blasts out of
tunnel closer, louder
trapped on the bridge

Quick! drop over the edge
clamp hands on railroad ties
dangle over Shoelace
grip, shiver and wait

Caboose passes
shivering its own timbers

At high noon wheels grind,
groan in canyon's tunnel
paging us front and center
to salute engineer's toot-toot.

Back inside to braid
rag rugs and card wool
until 4 o'clock
U.S. mail's whistle stop

Day fades night skies toss
mournful sighs at the stars
9:20 Main Liner rumbles past
dismissing us to upstairs room

To our two beds
three girls to a bed
giggles dwindle, disappear
into rhythmic breathing

2 a.m. Express moans
two sets of sleepy bodies
moan and shift in sync
sink in arms of Morpheus

Awaiting aromas and sounds
from the 6 o'clock Freighter

One stormy night Shoelace Creek flooded its bank within a few steps of our front porch. As water receded, we gleefully grabbed slippery, flopping fish with our bare hands. Our very own fish story.

"Eat hearty, fish is brain food!" So we did.

According to Lilas, Lois and Marilyn even better feasting came when the neighbor girl, Bernie, showed up each morning with a paper bag of leftover sourdough pancakes, without syrup. (This may account for Lilas's bent, years later, for snacking on cold boiled potatoes at the movies). Without a word to the adults, the little girls met Bernie on a bench under a huge tree, near Lilas's very own flourishing bed of

Zinnias, for their sourdough pancake picnic---without syrup, jam or butter.

It was no picnic, though, the morning we were met at the kitchen door by a slow-moving glacier of sourdough batter gone berserk. As usual we had "set" the sourdough before going to bed. During the night, the sourdough took on a life of it's own, bubbled out of the stone crock and slithered off the table and across the floor. Luckily, Ma knew how to start a new batch of sourdough starter.

Pedaling 'n Peddling

Pa quit his job on the Sheep Ranch near Preston, Minnesota to move us back to Chatfield before school started in September so we could be with our friends. After we loaded the truck, Velma and I devised a cozy sitting room with two rocking chairs among boxes, including that pink and green bedstead for the ride to the Sutherland house---our version of Steinbeck's Grapes of Wrath.

In this house each of us pedaled the treadles on our New Home sewing machine many miles to sew the latest fad---shirtwaist dresses with 16-gore skirts. See the picture of us holding the backs of our skirts fanned above our heads. Marilyn, Meredith and Lois—just the right size to kneel at strategic points behind us to support our skirt fans. No word what the reverse of this display looked like.

Those days all ladies wore slips, and those slips better have shadow panels, too, as no respectable lady would appear in public if one could see through her skirt (ala Princess Di's gossiped about photo). Crinoline petticoats flared out our dresses when we sat down, making us feel awfully prissy. Organdy and voile were popular fabrics for flattering dresses.

We pedaled that sewing machine treadle to sew aprons, often with embroidery trim. Bib aprons were worn for everyday around the house and garden. Savvy women sewed these with pump-handle pockets on the left side to avoid getting hung up while pumping soft water from the cistern or drawing drinking water at the windmill. Lefties placed their apron pockets accordingly. We sewed bib-less half aprons that tied at the waist, often trimmed with lace or embroidered designs for serving at church or community suppers. The easy way to look busy at these suppers was to wear an apron even though you may only be working the crowd. Other times, hats (with veils) and gloves were the uniform for properly dressed ladies.

One morning, a runny-nosed neighbor kid with his soft cap clapped down over his eyebrows wandered into our yard, tilted his chin up to assess our horses, saying "Dem yer hosses, Louie?" To this day we often describe a new hat to each other with "You know it's kind of a ' dem yer hosses, Louie" style.

From the Sutherland house we moved to the stone house an easy mile and half to school across Root River. Lilas remembers a steady diet of delicious homemade bread, plum sauce and milk for days and that really cold nights found us huddled on the floor at the top of the stairs to absorb heat from the stove downstairs.

Velma remembers how I found one more way to mortify her. Minnesota was throwing a pitch-black hissy fit of wind and rain making a trip to the backhouse unthinkable. None of us heard, or saw, Velma and her boyfriend drive up and park (necking) in the yard. Mother Nature prompted me to fling open the door and quickly squat in the ray of light from the house. Velma was mortified, wanted to die on the spot. I got off Scot free. Her boyfriend went to his grave with what they assumed was the image of being mooned by Mrs. Gehrke.

Soon it was Mr. Gehrke's turn to be embarrassed by me. He pastured a team of buckskin quarter horses behind the stone house. A girlfriend, Mina, and I rounded up Buck and Bright, bridled them and rode bareback down Main Street. His friends in town saw I had put the bridles on catty wampus. Don't ask. Serves me right, too, later Buck tripped and landed me in a ditch.

Sadly, the stone house has vanished, but not the memories. Builders dug too close to the foundation to build a basement and those magnificent stones sank—by now, may have become part of the Great Wall of China.

Donna seated, from left, Velma, me, Lilas

Homemade Bread and Pastries

To avoid another winter in the stone house, we moved to the Hoffman house at the edge of town where very early Saturday mornings, Pa turned his baking talent into homemade pastries: doughnuts (fried cakes), maple bars and sinfully frosted cinnamon rolls. Lilas and Lois were prettily outfitted with baskets over their arms for their route to waiting customers. Lois, three years younger, though taller than Lilas, took charge.

Lilas was the Elmer Blert "Nobody's home, I hope, I hope." kind of salesgirl, so when Lois emptied her basket, she'd help Lilas. They could have done without all the dogs in town trailing their tantalizing scents. Just when they had built up a large clientele, the local baker put them out of business—Pa's kitchen had no license. Lois huffed, "It's because our rolls were better than the baker's."

During one Saturday baking session baby of the family, preschooler

Meredith shuffled into the kitchen rubbing sleep from her eyes.

"I'd like a fresh doughnut, please."

Someone pointed to the table laden with a just-made batch. "Help yourself, little lady,"

Meredith picked up a doughnut, turned up her nose, "I mean a fresh one, this is not hot."

Lois took charge again the day she and Lilas threatened to set the house on fire. Towels hanging on a rack near the end of the wood-burning stove caught fire. Lilas whisked Marilyn and Meredith to the neighbors while Lois dumped a pan of water half full of potato peelings to douse the flames. It took all four of them to clean up the mess.

The next morning at sunrise, prowler noises came from the kitchen (no one in town locked their doors). Three-year-old Peggy Lou in her nightgown from up the street was helping herself to breakfast of homemade bread, lard and salt, none of which was served to her at home. She was the grocer's daughter, a playmate of Marilyn and Meredith. They had weaned Peggy on their original concoction of bread, lard and salt.

On the farm, preschoolers Lilas and Lois had enhanced their homemade bread and lard craze by raiding the gooseberry bushes. They came up with a tasty concoction by slicing gooseberries to top off their snack.

The aroma of bread baking was a constant in our home. "Whose turn is it to set the bread tonight?' was heard each Tuesday and Friday night. Wednesday baking was for bread only. Saturdays produced bread, cinnamon rolls and coffee cakes. Ma's hands flew like lightning to roll out and spice the dough as well as criss-cross designs with a knife atop the coffee cakes. For special treats, she let us frost the rolls.

As each girl grew tall enough to reach into the dishpan on a kitchen chair, to pull open the built-in tilt flour bin, to crank out five sifters of flour into the dish pan scooping out a hole in the middle of the flour heap, heat and measure a cup of water, and stir in a cake of dissolved yeast she had a turn on the bread-setting ritual. Making hills and valleys with the flour was jolly. Each batch made eight loaves.

The pity of it is, we didn't have enough sense to appreciate our school lunches of hand churned butter on homemade bread filled   with slices of seasoned sliced beef, pork or chicken. Instead, during lunchtime at school, we prowled to swap with kids with store-bought white bread and one slice of baloney or a scant layer of peanut butter. Duh!

A Clean Chimney, By Jimeny

Manitoba winds elbowed Pa in his ribs as he studied the gunmetal sky the fall of 1935. We lived in the Sutherland house up the slope from the dead end of the railroad tracks at the edge of Chatfield, population 1214.

He nodded my way, cocked his head raising his eyebrows with "The chimney needs cleaning, are you game?"

His was a question, not a parental command. Our only brother, Paul, was away and at 12 years I was the oldest daughter available. Cleaning the chimney meant climbing on the roof of our three-story house. That sounded scary and exciting. Why not? So I did.

"Sure, what do I have to do?"

"For starters, get into these," he handed over a pair of overalls plucked from the ragbag, his weathered jacket, and a stocking cap.

Ma supervised the buttoning all the way up to my chin and tied a muffler over my mouth and nose. Patting my shoulder she giggled, "You look good enough to rob one of the banks in town." They grinned, gave me a look of approval and helped me pull on Paul's hobnail boots and leather gloves.

We clumped upstairs to the back porch roof as a handy step to climb up to the pinnacle of the house. That same porch roof had often made for comfortable sleeping on sticky summer nights when we sisters lugged our mattresses out there. In this snow country roofs are slanted. I still wonder that not one girl rolled over in her sleep to land in the tomato patch two stories below.

With heavy cable hooked to a fat, fuzzy rope and a log chain, I was checked out on our plan.

"Keep a tight grip on the cable, climb to the chimney and *very* slowly lower the rope and chain down the chimney until you feel me tug on it from the furnace in the basement."

He hoisted me over the eaves of the house roof reminding me to let him do the swinging---to keep from chipping bricks on the chimney wall. My only job was to keep a grip on the cable. I fell to my hands and knees dragging the cable, rope and chain up to the chimney. He waited until I was firmly in place straddling the roof.

He cautioned, "You know now how heavy that log chain is, so be ready for the jerk of its weight when you first drop it down the chimney." I nodded.

He turned and headed down the three flights to the basement, his voice fading, "Close your eyes tight and keep a grip on the cable."

Then I felt his gentle tug from below. Eyes squeezed shut, I gripped. I waited. The cable twitched. It swung slowly. Soot flew. I gripped. The wind blew. The chimney swayed. More gentle swinging. My eyes squeezed tighter. I gripped harder.

None too soon his voice echoed through the chimney. "Good Girl. Don't move. Stay right where you are until I come up to help you down."

The sound of him unhooking and dropping the chain echoed. I hugged the chimney. He stepped on the porch roof and assured me it was safe to pull up the rope. That part was easy with the chain now unhooked.   With the rope heaped on the roof beside me, I tossed the end of the cable toward him. He pulled the cable and rope and dropped them to the garden path.

With him poised to catch me, sliding down the roof was a piece of cake. I landed safely in his arms sending up a fume of soot from our clothes. We burst out laughing. Only the whites of our eyes looked like us.

Well, by Jimeny, that was fun. What next? Ma grinned, "Why not take on a   more down-to-earth challenge?"

So I did. Girl friends had taken up archery, I bought a 40-lb bow to aim at a target set up on our side yard where just below the railroad tracks came to a dead end.

Hobos waiting for the next train to back into town were as much at risk of bleeding from a misfired arrow, than my bleeding left wrist was until I got the hang of sending off that arrow.

Perms, Primping and Pastels

Each time Frieda brought out her barber shears and clippers in the 1920's and 30's, any of her nine daughters under 10 years old would end up with a buster brown haircut. Her preordained tradition squelched arguments and speculations on who might look good with particular hairstyles that we admired in mail order catalogs. With the kitchen or the back porch as her barbershop, each customer draped in a discarded tablecloth sat on the backless kitchen stool. Her scissors fashioned bangs and the hand-operated clippers laid down smooth shingles up the backs of our heads.

Brother Paul was spared the buster brown cut. Not before his 16th birthday had he had a haircut by the real barber in town. Her skill never tormented Paul with a "bowl" haircut, though it's true, that an "ouch" or "oops" could be heard now and again above the sound of the clippers. She never drew blood.

By the time eldest sister Helen was a teenager, she developed into a proficient hairdresser to be recruited by each of us the minute we turned ten. When Toni home permanents came on the market, we pooled our savings to buy one bottle of permanent solution and neutralizer to stretch this into three perms in one smelly session. Three of us shampooed and set up an assembly line with one standing to start the process on the girl sitting on a chair who then continued on the third girl sitting on the floor clamped between the sitter's knees, each standing or sitting on the floor or chair as the process timing called for.

In the 1920's, we envied hired girl, Eleanor, who lucked out with naturally wavy hair. Before her boyfriend was due for a date, she'd primp by holding her head over the steaming teakettle spout shaping waves with her fingers into her luxurious black hair.

When hired girl, cousin Edna, got ready for her dates with Alvin, we fluttered around her dressing table, leaning on our elbows to watch her apply make up. Her face powder box seemed the size of a soup bowl and the huge puff sent loose powder flying with a flourish of her wrist that made us sneeze. No blush brushes in those days, but she took the tiny puff pad from her compact to rouge her cheeks, pulling faces at herself in the mirror. Pongee lipstick finished the job and we left her bedroom feeling properly tutored on big-girl stuff.

Theirs was our first chance to see a rainbow wedding. Edna in white surrounded by a maid of honor and bridesmaids each dressed in a different pastel. Watching these gowns float down the aisle sent us to fairyland. Our beloved Edna had often amused us with silly ditties. A favorite was using each of our names to recite:

Donna Tonna Kulla Wulla Wonna,
Kulla Wulla Winktem Tinktem Ponna

Beginning with Helen Tellen Kulla Wulla Wellen, down the line to, Velma Telma,

Bernice Ternice, Lilas Tilas...delighted and taught us to sing-song through all ten of our names ending with the baby of the family, Meredith Teredith. Paul Taul Kulla Walla Waul, Kulla Wulla Winktem Tinktem Paul was the easiest and we decided made the most sense.

While good grooming was stressed, we were brought to our senses when Father shook his head with a wink, "powder and paint makes a girl think she's something she ain't."

After a Buster-Brown session, Velma, Helen, Bernice, Donna, Baby Paul and Me

Amateur Shows and Choirs

We sisters often sang between acts in trios or mixed quartets when the youth group at church produced three-act plays. Since only Velma played piano with two hands, we'd practice at home with two or three sitting on the piano bench, each picking out her own part singing along. Not a pretty sound. One of our favorites, "Whispering Hope" could have used more whispering.

This same youth group of two dozen teens regularly attended Sunday night hockey games downtown St. Paul. We arrived early to claim our favorite general admission seats and get our socializing in before the game. Once the puck was dropped we concentrated on our star player Bobby Orr and tried to keep Velma from being arrested. At one game her exuberance got away from her, she screamed at the officials, lifted the hat off a man in front of her and clamped it down over his face. We pretended not to notice when this stranger turned around.

Monday nights, our home on Victoria Street soon fell to the brink of disgrace with our impromptu "talent" shows. The den, behind French doors off the living room, was backstage where two or three quickly hatched mimes, songs, dances, recitations or dramatizations to present to each other. As soon as word got out of these shenanigans, girlfriends, Buzzie, Florence and Jenny found excuses for a sleep over on Mondays. Buzzie considered our home her second home, even though, now at 88 years, she still grumbles about never gaining priority to sleep in the middle, landing her on the floor during the night now and again.

During one trumped up mime by Lois and me, Velma clutched her stomach, rolled on the floor in a fit of laughter and tears begging for mercy until Lois and I got a grip on our selves and left the stage. Neither of us admits to remembering the mime. Did I mention that our parents arranged never to be home on Monday nights?

Not all our performances were of such low caliber. In high school Donna and I sang in a girls' quartet at funerals. Donna, Velma and I sewed look-a-like dresses to sing at a friend's wedding. Helen sang in the High School girls' octet and we all sang in choruses to win first place in the state musical festival competitions for several successive years. Later, several of us auditioned for, and were accepted in touring A Capella concert choirs. Velma rose to the level of directing the children's choir, and wrote music for them on special occasions. Marilyn and Meredith sang in school and church choirs and felt privileged to be accompanied by a professional harpist, Lorraine King.

While trying to harmonize, I sometimes heard, "You can't sing worth sour apples." To disprove this oft-repeated critique, I sneaked to tryouts for the prestigious Twin Cities A Capella Choir directed by the internationally famous Paul Manz. Following my tryout the panel said, "Thank you for coming, we'll call you." Two or three sisters had also tried out. Our phone rang and a man's voice asked for Ann to attend the first rehearsal. Velma said, "You've got the wrong girl. You can't mean Ann." The man meant Ann. My secret was out. Shock and mortification set in for those sisters not called back. Nyah, nyah, nyah time for me. Blending my voice with other second altos produced sounds I didn't know were in me. Our first performance had me feeling woozy until intermission when I relaxed enough to unlock my knees.

Lilas sang the lead role in the high school productions of "Rose of the Danube" and "In Old Vienna" in which Lois sang to play Lilas's mother. The next year Lois fell in love with her male lead in "Waltz Dream" who asked her to the prom. At the same time a farmer boy friend from out of town sent her a dozen roses. Sorting through her boyfriends amused us. One night at dinner, she slapped the table, "I'll never marry a farmer, they work too hard, never get a day off, and always have to go home early to do the chores." Less than six months later, at that same dinner table, she announced her engagement to Harold, the only farmer in the family. Six children, 19 grandchildren, 5 great-grandchildren and 60 years later they retired from going home early to do the chores.

Lois, Lilas and Nora (brother Paul's future wife) are the trio singing on a tape sealed in the cornerstone of a large Minneapolis church, Lilas sang with the All-City Robert Shaw Chorale, and her high school choir regularly entertained troops stopping at the St. Paul train depot in the 1940's.

Paul was asked to sing scales for Miss Nelson, the music teacher. She was delighted to find a good male tenor. He was proving a favorite old saw "Cry at your baptism, grow up to be a good choir member." True, he slid up and down the scales pure as you please and the melody went well; but forget harmony. In rehearsal he was seated between two girl tenors to help him get the hang of harmonizing. No dice, he heard only the melody. Miss Nelson frowned, "Paul, could you just mouth words for the performance?" He said, "Okay, as long as the two girls stay."

Paul played trombone in B Band. For Christmas vacation he had been assigned to learn two pieces. First day back the band director, Mr. Arsers, met him in the band room in the basement of the school. Paul opened the trombone case—it was moldy. Mr. Arsers asked, "You going to play trombone or play football? Paul was swayed by the successes of Bernie Bierman as head coach of the Minnesota Gophers. The trombone lost. Football didn't take all of his time; he had taken time to keep secret that he had entered a speech contest. Just before his performance Velma heard about the competition and slipped into the auditorium to see and hear him. At dinner that night she announced, "You should have heard Paul win a prize at the declamatory contest today."

Living Without Nylons and Elastic

Our family guarded a fistful of ration books to keep us in flour, sugar, coffee, and clothes during World War II. One by one the war scattered cousins and neighbors enlisting in service around the country. Paul saw the world as a Merchant Marine. I worked in a defense plant in Minneapolis, Velma and Donna found work in St. Paul followed soon by our parents and the little girls.

Little sisters, Lilas, Lois, Marilyn and Meredith, were still in knee socks, but keeping the legs of us older girls in nylon stockings drove us to the edge of crime. We're not talking about just any legs. In the 1930's Helen and Bee each had won the annual prettiest-legs competitions in Chatfield High School and Velma had displayed her shapely gams representing Richter's Drug Store in a beauty contest.

Alas, the wartime shortage of nylons left our legs bare. After we moved to St. Paul, penciling a line up the backs of our bare legs to simulate seams of nylon stockings was cold comfort and didn't cut it fashion-wise. Neither did slathering makeup on our legs which kept us avoiding puddles of water or slush. Getting caught in the rain gave away our beauty tricks while makeup streaked and dribbled into our shoes. What a mess.

We prowled department stores on weekends, after school, after work, and on lunch hours sniffing out even the slightest rumor that nylons were about to show up at hosiery counters. We joined long lines and recruited our father and uncles to stand in line for us at Schunemann's Department Store's lingerie counters. These lines often spilled into the street. The supply of nylons always ran out with people still in line bringing up a roar, "What do you mean there are no more nylons? We've been standing here for two hours." These outbursts made us giddy.

For sport, we sisters formed our own lines at department store counters with not a clue that nylons were available. As soon as several customers had been conned into lining up behind our fake line the sister at the head shrugged, feigned impatience and gave up her spot. One by one we dropped off the head of the line to gather on the mezzanine to peek through the rail enjoying the havoc we had wreaked for the badgered salesgirl. When Bee, our sensible, now married sister, overheard us giggling about our pranks she shamed us into going straight with, "Think of the sacrifices by the women and men in our military."

More serious than our bare legs was the shortage of elastic, making us, and all women, nervous when forced to rely on buttoned waistbands to keep undergarments in place. One Sunday morning after a heavy snowstorm that kept cars off all residential streets, we hiked home from church with a dozen and a half other teenage and adult parishioners. Bundled in heavy winter clothing, including snow boots nearly to our knees, we made the most of this chance to slip and slide in the nearly deserted streets while throwing snowballs. Snowplows had cleared streetcar tracks on University Avenue in St. Paul.

"Help me," whispered sister #4, Donna, reaching for my arm. She had hoisted her right boot to step across the slick streetcar tracks at the very instant the crucial button popped off. Her panties draped at half mast over her boots, hobbling her.

A streetcar came. The motorman pulled the warning whistle cord to clear the tracks, alerting all fellow hikers to turn around in time to witness Donna's predicament. Several of us, smothering laughter, lifted her and tugged the offending garment to un-hobble her. Freed with undraped boots, she crammed the panties in her pocket and strode home acknowledging with a bow the applause for her grace under pressure.

That Time of the Month

"Dinner's ready, bring your purses," would float up to our bedroom in St. Paul, interrupting us girls changing from school or work clothes. Now and again the call might also echo down the basement stairwell, where one of us might be rinsing out tomorrow's slip and panties or developing film in the washtubs.

"Oh, Fiddle, it's that time of the month again", we mumbled. We dropped what we were doing, bundled our purses to the dining room table to sit at our places designated by the personal napkin rings we each had crocheted.

Sitting-down noises faded and heads bowed for "Come Lord Jesus,..." followed by clinking silverware with bowls and platters passing that competed with prattle to swap news, check dates and with whom. Well fed, our gossip, grandiose plans and giggles simmered to a stop.

It was time for "Give thanks to the Lord..." followed by a volley of purses snapping open to display folding money and clanking change. Out came receipts, sales slips and scribbles on paper scraps to settle up our month's borrowing and lending for car fare, movie tickets, lipstick, mascara, spur-of-the-moment dress or hat purchases, maybe last Sunday's offering plate or board and room from the wage-earning girls.

This Peter-to-Pay-Paul merry-go-round played to a tune that went something like "Anybody got change for a dollar or two nickels for a dime, okay if I owe you ' til payday...?" In the end, much of this fluttering cash landed back in the purse from whence it came. Suzi Ormand would've been proud.

Everybody's Good for Something

In 1960 in a sweaty huff, five-year-old Jane blew through our front door in Chandler, Arizona and flounced into her favorite rocking chair declaring, "You're right, Mommy, 'everybody' s good for something'—even if it's a bad example." I tried not to smile as she let off a stream of steam about Marjory, her best friend down the street.

Jane rode that rocking chair with stern purpose. After a few cooler huffs and puffs, she sighed, slid off her perch, smiled and headed back to Marjory's. There should be a Nobel Peaceful Prize for the inventor of rocking chairs.

Beginning with my sister Helen's birth on July 29,1918, my eight sisters and one brother each began life feeling the peace of a rocking chair as Grandma Krumdieck ladled sugar water between our tiny lips. She sat at the foot of Frieda's birthing bed on our Minnesota farm. It may well be

Grandma's *fault* that when life finally brought indoor plumbing to our family, a rocking chair became a standard fixture in our bathrooms along with tub, sink and toilet. Oh, that today's bathrooms were that roomy!

Actually, outdoor plumbing on the farm sported a three-holer---two adult and one child---setting our pace of restroom sociability as soon as each of us was out of diapers.

Indoors, rocking chairs make for a pleasant ambiance while waiting for turns to use your choice(s) of the facilities. Suppose we sisters can be blamed for starting the universal habit of women visiting the restroom in droves? And, visiting is just what we did while rocking and bathing away our secret sins and sharing dreams. We savored having someone handy to scrub our backs followed by the luxury of body lotion being artfully applied to that spot between our shoulders. We taught each other how to shave legs and underarms, to do manicures and pedicures. We set and combed out each other's hair into latest styles. Two or three faces being made up at the same moment in the bathroom mirror sometimes let me believe I really was the one with naturally curly hair.

When we moved to St. Paul, we girls painted the bathroom. The robin-egg blue looked so good on the walls that the rocking chair got a coat of paint, too.

When Pa called up the stairs, "How soon can I have the bathroom to clean up and shave?" Mischief overtook us. After a few minutes, we opened the door calling, "Okay, the bathroom is ready for you to clean up and comb your hair—both of them." He grinned at his smart aleck daughters, walked through the bathroom door and howled with laughter looking at the mirror painted blue, too.

During our growing up years, and before automatic dishwashers, we easily fell into lovely tell-all gab sessions while washing dishes up to our elbows in soothing hot, soapy water. What a pity that automatic dishwashers took away this togetherness that had kept us communicating in a comfortable space until the washing and drying were finished. Snapping towels was not allowed, "You could put out someone's eye."

In May of 2010, that long-lost sister intimacy came back when 88-year-old Donna, 13 months older than I and Lilas, four years younger, were my houseguests. I needed a bath and a shampoo. The rocking chair doesn't fit in my Oakmont Village guest bath. Inviting Donna to sit on the throne lid and Lilas on the tiny table housing toiletries served nicely for our chance to get back to the good old days. Neither has lost her touch for scrubbing a back and applying lotion or giving a pedicure.

Our individual talents and inclinations were in plain sight during childhood and have continued through family reunions as kitchen assignments fall in place without fanfare.

Cleanup duty was assigned to me after I suggested Jello on the Half Shell. Cooking charmed my sisters and kept us well fed. However, not-too-subtle hinting always had steered our late sister, Bee, to "Please stay clear of the coffee pot."

Everybody'   s good for something, be it a bad example----or building rocking chairs.

Hand-Me-Down Men

Growing up in hand-me-down clothes made our habit of handing down boyfriends common---not the men, the habit. With nine girls ripe for the picking; our phone number 0039 was easy. The girls were not.

While sorting through the men, dating and courting evolved into competition to be the first couple home in the evening for squatter's rights in the living room or den to entertain boyfriends. Minnesota winters cut short bidding goodnight on the front door stoop, glazed porch or in the car; though neighbors on the farm, and later in St. Paul, did remark on the steady stream of cars with steamy windows parked at our house.

Our parents prohibited our dating any boyfriend who pulled up on his bike, calling out the name of his choice, or sat in his car honking the horn. "Come to the door, Buster, or forget it,"

Helen handed off at least one boyfriend to Velma and Bee dated one of Helen's hand-me-downs. Donna and I handed back and forth a boyfriend who escaped into the ministry. One man was tested by three of us. Sometimes men showed up at our door on the hunch at least one girl would be available. If not, they pulled up a chair and visited with our parents. Marilyn and Meredith, referred to as the 'little girls', escaped these hand-me-downs; however, Marilyn and Lois each married men named Harold Anderson, adding to our confusion.

Swapping men slowed down after settling on which boyfriend was whose. The minute Bee was permitted to date, Hans turned his attention from Helen and never looked back. Wednesday, Friday and Saturday nights he saddled his mare, Trixie, galloped across grain fields and wooded hills with his violin under his arm. He and that fiddle made beautiful music. His signature piece was "Twas on the Isle of Capri that I Met Her." Bee answered on the piano with "Over the Waves." When he proposed, we teased that her affliction of stammering stalled her answer long enough for Hans to take her silence as "Yes." Helen was maid of honor, Velma played the church's pump organ, Donna sang.I had my first chance as bridesmaid.

My boyfriend was working his way through law school in a reupholster shop when Bee asked him to reupholster their couch. Pulling taut the fabric, spitting tacks and hammering a mile a minute he slipped and tacked his thumb to the couch. Aghast at the sight of blood, Bee sputtered, "What should I do?" He uttered, "Glass of water, please." She brought the water, looked at his bleeding thumb, felt faint, drank the water herself and slumped on the couch with him still tacked to it. He married me anyway, amid processions of nine brides and one groom over the years.

But that's another book.

Pine Tree Pride

In the 1920's and 30's on the farm, early each December after school, already dark, Bee, Donna, Paul and I stomped across fields to sell Christmas Seals to the neighbors assigned to us by the teacher. An okay chore, but the really big deal was baking Christmas cookies. The year I was in fourth grade, cousin Melvin decorated a gingerbread cookie with an arrow through Ralph's and my name.

Delight and embarrassment flushed my face down to my toes, all the while protesting, "I don't like Ralph anyway, even if he did give me a bottle of Ben Hur."

I paid for my sham a few days later when three-year-old Lois poured the perfume into the chamber pot "because you don't like Ralph anyway."

Lois remembers during particularly hard times when Miss Gallagher asked her if she had a nice Christmasy dress to recite, ' The Night Before Christmas' in a school program?" Lois said, "yes," then came home to admit fibbing. She asked to borrow a red plaid pleated skirt from Lilas, three years older, but shorter. Lois performed. Lilas wasn't in the program anyway.

It had been our source of pride that Christmas trees for the school, the church, and the parlor came from the windbreak west of the house on our farm. Pine trees stretched behind the sheep shed, corncrib, and well house and in front of the grove of oaks, elms, and butternut trees.

Each December, lighted ladyfinger candles in glistening clip-on holders clung to the woodsy smelling Christmas tree. Holiday traditions followed us no matter in which growing-up house we lived. In the 1920's and 30's each night through the week before Christmas, our father sat beside the tree with a pail of water and a rag mop, concentrating on the candles while his son and daughters concentrated on speaking our recitations.

Bible verses had been assigned to each of us during Saturday morning rehearsals at church for the Children's Christmas Eve program. At home, we performed to an audience of our parents, siblings, the hired man (Fred, Hans or Glen), and the hired girl (Edna or Eleanor) who sat on dining room chairs in the arch doorway between the dining room and parlor. They applauded and coached us to speak with expression.

After we recited our pieces, rehearsal began for all verses of carols from "Away in a Manger" on through "Silent Night" with Frieda at the pump organ keeping us on key. Then we were shooed to bed, our excitement at fever pitch.

Many of these recitations became part of the County District 98 Christmas school program along with skits, monologues and carols directed by Miss Perry, later Miss Kretschmar, in our one-room eight-grades country school. The Friday evening before Christmas a curtain hung on metal hooks along a wire strung across the front rows of the pupils' desks. Beside the pump organ with an ornate mirror on top, the Christmas tree oozed fragrance and glory from left stage, while the cloakroom on stage right became backstage.

A choice assignment, when not performing, was monitor at the cloak room door to make sure each child was costumed and ready to go on stage at the right moment. The year I was assigned the honor of monitor my face tingled with a sappy smile. I never did get to pull the curtain, a job that also carried prestige. Our adoring audience (waiting to be proud or humiliated by turn) of parents, cousins, aunts, uncles, grandparents, and neighbors wedged into our school desks or borrowed folding chairs. Men of broad girth or long legs leaned against the schoolroom's side and back walls.

Come Christmas Eve, the men hitched up Rex and Hector---each a ton of ever-ready power with magnificent fetlock feathers glistening with tiny snowballs. They laid down parallel sleigh tracks across our snow-crusted lawn to the back porch door. We scrambled onto the sleigh atop horse blankets covering a bed of clean straw and cuddled under cowhides with green felt edging and our own bed quilts, careful not to wrinkle our new Christmas outfits during the eight-mile ride to church in Chatfield.

One Christmas Eve, three-year-old sister, Bee, proudly standing beside the tree from *our* farm, won the hearts of the congregation by fidgeting with her dress while she spoke her piece. Coyly twisting, she gathered her skirt to her underarms to display her long underwear and home-sewn Christmas petticoat with ruffles designed from flour sacks with "Gold Medal" bleached out.

All recitations spoken, all carols sung, all prayers prayed, elders of the church came forward to present each child with a bag of hard Christmas candy, nuts, and an orange. Our childish pride spiked on the years that those oranges were courtesy of our Aunt Elma and Uncle Otto, who had shipped them from their home in The Rio Grande Valley in Texas.

Clutching our candy and fruit we went behind the church where Rex and Hector snorted as they were un-blanketed and re-hitched. We climbed into the sleigh, teeth chattering and snuggled under the blankets. The team turned toward home while our excitement, impromptu caroling, and chatter about who recited our Christmas piece with the most expression faded into the darkness where only the moon and stars could see us for eight miles.

Village lights slid off the world
Stars appeared haphazardly hurled

When we heard "Time to wake up. We're home," the team pulled through the wide gate of the yard onto the lawn to the back door. We piled out taking our bed blankets inside with us. When the men came in from putting the team to bed, bowls of oyster stew with tiny round oyster crackers were ready, hoping to put a lid on the built-up anticipation about what Santa had brought. That set of play dishes found at Donna and my places is still in my cedar Hope Chest.

On to Frieda and Louis who started all of this.

Frieda's Posturing

Away with those ladyfinger-like candles when we left behind our precious windbreak of Christmas trees. We moved to town, to electricity. In a twinkling, we turned into art critics. Stringing lights on the store-bought tree had us stepping off the kitchen stool, stepping back, squinting--- all but standing on one's head. Then it was "more lights lower on that branch– too many lights on top..." Unscrewing and rearranging bulbs to achieve color coordination had us taking turns to step outside to view our spectacle from the street---never mind that one might land in a snowdrift or slip on ice.

Debates on swapping blue for green, red for yellow continued through the 12 days of Christmas to Epiphany, when we heard: "bring the boxes to store the ornaments–careful not to tangle the strings of lights." We inhaled the waning scent of pine and brushed away needles.

Weeks before Christmas, Frieda took up unlady postures under the tree to rattle, shake and squeeze gifts. Sometimes she expertly opened and re-wrapped her own gifts. We kept secret our gifts to her, camouflaging the wrappings. One year in St. Paul, she hinted, "I could use a nighty." Each of us was *sure* no one else would take her bold hint. The first gift she opened was a nighty, then a second nighty. Quizzical glances darted around the room, then broad smiles broke into hilarity by the time she opened the sixth nightgown. She returned not one of them.

One Christmas Eve she was IT for our clap game. She was sent out of the room while we decided that we would clap her into her usual snooping posture on her hands and knees behind the Christmas tree, which stood at the bay window. The closer she got, the louder we clapped. Next morning the neighbor man came to ask why our mother was on the floor behind the Christmas tree. During the holidays we never closed the curtains on the tree stood.

We walked about a dozen blocks to church, with our parents being careful to be well ahead of, or behind, us lest people realize they were part of that giggling group. On Christmas Eve, we attended early services for the little girl's choir, walked home for gift opening and games, then back to candlelight service for the older girls' choir. After midnight, home for oyster stew to settle us in for a quick night's sleep before returning for Christmas Day services. Who knows how many walk-a-thons we covered for weekly services, choir practice, play practice, and youth meetings day or night? We took comfort in, "There's safety in numbers."

Apart from our own work-up ball games we had played on the farm and the constant physical labor of farming, our parents not only danced for exercise, they encouraged us to use a chinning bar installed in the doorway between the kitchen and dining room. The bar had notches at several heights to accommodate any size adult or child. Good posture was tended to,

"Stand straight", "Don't slouch, shoulders back." We gave a whirl at trying to carry books on our heads. Frieda competed with us to touch the backs or the palms of our hands behind our backs. She was really good at it.

She devised her own sneaky system for getting us up each morning. Whether is was 6:05, 6;30 or 6:55 she'd calmly call upstairs, "Wake up, girls, it's going on 7." We couldn't trust her one bit to announce accurate time. But, it worked.

One afternoon, several sisters and she were visiting while half seated at the edge of the dining room table. Suddenly with frivolity, she swung her legs up to land her feet on the sewing machine cabinet not missing a beat in the conversation. Small wonder that she was active within several months of her death at age 75.

Her upbeat attitude made it acceptable for Lois to show up in a bright red dress at Mother's funeral in Colorado. In the ante room of the church before the service, Lois from Minnesota sidled up to me whispering, "How did I know this Colorado funeral director would ask us to remove our coats?" She removed her black coat. Like a beacon, she marched in red with the rest of us dressed in black to the front of the church.

Actually, Lois's red dress gave us the giggles in the limo enroute to the cemetery and again a few hours later as we gathered in Velma's rec room in the basement to choose mementos which Frieda "had the good sense" to lay out on the ping-pong table in orderly fashion, "the way God intended it"– two of her fond expressions.

Louis' Quirks and Quips

"Hire a hall," was his polite version of "shut up" whenever our voices drifted across the hall to their bedroom in St. Paul. Until then, their bedrooms had been on the first floor where they had been spared from our bedtime commotion.

"Use your head, it's not just a hat rack," he encouraged with a smile, when a daughter or son came for help to work through a knotty gadget, or a hitch in math or English homework. Once he wrote an intriguing short story of a lady's sleek legs and graceful neck—then surprised us when it turned out to be a perfect description of our mare, Lady.

He whistled while he worked, indoors or outdoors. He whumped up the best ever breakfasts in the whole world. The oven perching beside the old-style gas stove burners made a handy shelf to keep warm his plate of bacon, eggs over easy, toast from homemade bread and his cup of coffee that meant business. While he turned to pour his coffee his breakfast usually disappeared. He feigned surprise, shrugged and called around the corner into the dining room where his light-fingered daughters, already late for work or school, were wolfing down his breakfast.

"You think this is your birthday or something?" he'd say turning to come up with another breakfast. Most mornings this happened at least twice, one morning his plate disappeared six times. He shrugged, "What's your hurry?"

Each of us had a different excuse. He pulled out one of his tired old saws, "Early to bed, early to rise makes a girl healthy, wealthy and wise." We just groaned.

If one of us appeared wearing red and yellow, we heard, "Red and yellow, catch a fellow." We groaned.

"Homely in the cradle, pretty at the table," seeing pouty faces of whimpering babies. Or, "Cry at your baptism, sing in the choir."

"Curly sky won't keep 24 hours dry," using his farmer's feel for reading the sky and the wind. More groaning.

One morning he tweaked our groaning while he worked over a hot frying pan, whistling and keeping time with the spritzing bacon, he sing-songed, "It's folly, and it's crude to fry bacon in the nude." Laughter choked our groans.

In June of 1957 my own family was packing to move from Colorado to Oregon. I sat beside his hospital bed for goodbyes adding, "Maybe I can be back before Thanksgiving."

He chuckled. "Maybes don't fly in June." I giggled took his hands in mine and recited a hymn verse. (I didn't sing, for heaven sake, the man was already in enough pain). He recited with me.

Blest be the tie that binds
our hearts in Christian love.
When here our pathways part,
we suffer bitter pain, yet,
one in Christ and one in heart,
we know we'll meet again.
Amen.

On September 27, 1957 the sad word
reached me by phone. I blubbered,
"What's your hurry?"

After word

It's time again to slide between cozy sheets to mourn and give thanks to Lady---the driving force that brought Louis Gehrke and Frieda Krumdieck together to create our family.

The Gehrke Family
1943

Acknowledgements.

Kudos to Ralph Morin of Malibu for assembling the finished layout of this book.

Thanks to Ellen Reich and her group of Malibu writers whose creativity and enthusiastic support hooked me on writing poetry and memoirs; and to the Oakmont Village writers led by James Fitch and Suzanne Sherman for their encouragement and editorial expertise.

Thanks to computer tutors Dick and Gloria Salander, Pat Barclay, Jud Goodrich, Eddy Jacobs, Marshall Lee, Bob Stinson, and Kate McCullough for their time and patience.

Apologies to anyone omitted.

7379473R0

Made in the USA
Charleston, SC
25 February 2011